OVER THE TOP

SOLUTIONS TO THE SISYPHUS DILEMMAS OF LIFE

......as told by
Billy Gamble

By

William N. Thompson, Ph. D.
Bradley L. Kenny, J.D.

1st Books Library
Bloomington, IN
2003

This book is a work of fiction. Places, events, and situations in this story are purely fictional. Any resemblance to actual persons, living or dead, is coincidental.

ISBN: 1-4033-9135-1 (e-book)
ISBN: 1-4033-9136-X (Paperback)
ISBN: 0-7596-1172-6 (Dustjacket)

Library of Congress Control Number: 2002095521

This book is printed on acid free paper.

Printed in the United States of America
Bloomington, IN

1stBooks - rev. 2/13/03

ACKNOWLEDGMENTS

So many friends and acquaintances over so many years have provided us with materials that have found a way into this book. We acknowledge with gratitude their help in sharing and also their encouragement. Having such friends is a very essential element in coping with trials and tribulations and overcoming the same in our all too often Sisyphus style lives. We are especially thankful for the assistance received from Laura Thompson and from members of the Craig Kenny and Associates Law Firm in Las Vegas. We enjoy the memories of fun together in New Orleans. We are also very grateful for the photographic skills of Marty Dowling and the staff of 1st Books Library, especially Vid Beldavs, Marsha McCrosskey, Jon Spencer.

DEDICATION

To Sean, Steve, Tim, and Laura, our children.
They've struggled often with the rocks and
mountains that we may have placed in
their pathways. We only hope that
in these pages we may be able to
share some solutions for the
Sisyphus dilemmas that
we have given
to them.

TABLE OF CONTENTS

INTRODUCTION

If your life feels like:

- You are going ninety miles an hour down a dead-end street...
- The best that you can hope for is to die in your sleep...
- What goes up must always come down...
- You are just spinning wheels but getting nowhere...
- You are constantly reinventing the wheel...
- For each step forward you are taking two steps backwards...
- You are hitting your head against a brick wall...
- You are always going back to square one...
- You are living the definition of insanity, doing the same things over and over and expecting different results...
- You are living the gambler's prayer: "Lord, tonight let me break even, I really need the money..."
- You are pushing big rocks up a mountain, only to see them roll back down again...over and over

...then the story of Sisyphus may be your story too.

Then you should explore opportunities to break the patterns of frustration that surround so much of your existence. Get ready to roll. It is time that you complete your journey. Get ready to go **OVER THE TOP**.

In classical literature the character of Sisyphus got his "just deserts." He was a minor league trickster who played around a little too much in the big leagues. Characters the likes of Zeus and Hades did not care for the games he played, and when they finally captured him, they assigned to him his fate. For eternity he would push a big rock up a mountain. However, just as he was about to reach the peak and achieve the goal of pushing the rock over the top, it would slip from his hands and roll back down. He would then have to go back down, retrieve the rock, and begin the push anew, only to realize the same results. For eternity, now, he has been pushing that rock.

His story is a metaphor for modern organizational living. We are all pushing rocks. Can we achieve another result, or are we condemned to push rocks for eternity never to achieve our goals? This book examines the Sisyphus dilemmas of our lives, and this book suggests ways of coping with our rocks and our mountains so that we may achieve a contentment in our tasks, but also so that we may achieve an accomplishment of results—so that we may see the rock go **OVER THE TOP**. And when it does, we will be CELEBRATING our victory, be it a large one or a small one.

CHAPTER 1

LAISSEZ LES BON TEMPS ROULER: INVITATION TO NEW ORLEANS

Semester break at the University of Nevada, Las Vegas (UNLV), is usually a void reserved for relaxation and maybe a few days of skiing in southern Utah. In 2001 it was different. I was invited to New Orleans by my friend Frederick Walker for a retreat gathering of his friends, and members of his firm. Fred had been one of my best students as an undergraduate at UNLV. He thought that perhaps I could share part of my public administration thinking with his friends, as they and his legal partners examined progress in their work lives. I was quite pleased that he wanted to show-off a professor from his alma mater to his friends, and that I was that professor.

Fred made the invitation sweeter by indicating that they would stay around until the start of Mardi Gras, and that they would also take in several restaurants and other sights, including the casino. My friend, who had done quite well with his firm, Walker and Hardcastle, Associates, rented an entire bed and breakfast on St. Charles Avenue. I looked forward to the streetcar rides. I was especially happy to spend a week in New Orleans as my daughter Jennifer was working at Loyola University as a Residential Life counselor. Fred told me he wanted to include Jennifer in some of the events, especially group discussions about motivation.

CHAPTER 2

WE ARRIVE AND DO THE BLUEBIRD CAFE

Several of the group arrived at the New Orleans airport on Wednesday morning. We were picked up by Eddie Bauschard, Fred's classmate from his law school days at Tulane. We went to the bed and breakfast—the ole Mansion d'le Jardin—and crashed for an hour or so, when the next group came in and started yelling about doing breakfast at the Bluebird Cafe on Prytania Street. Fred shouted for everyone to hear—"Professor Billy Gamble is here, all is right with the world, time to get up and go. It is time to rock and roll."

After only a few minutes, six of us were walking the four blocks to the cafe. There we saw the lineup of about 20 people on the sidewalk, and we became part of their numbers. The doorman greeted each of us, and we noticed that he was also greeting many of the guests by their names. He kept his eye on the various guests, and he made sure that they were invited in the door in the order that they had arrived. He also told us the approximate waiting time was fifteen minutes.

When we were seated fourteen minutes later, we understood more reasons for the success of this Prytania Street landmark. Service was timely and friendly, the food was well prepared and tasty, and the cost was what one would expect to pay in a cafe serving a local neighborhood. That is, it was quite reasonable. The Bluebird also featured many photographs and souvenirs of life in New Orleans—actually the place was a miniature museum.

Day after day those who worked at the Bluebird Cafe did the same thing, only to go home, then come back the next day for more of the same. Never once did any employee or member of the management team suggest to us that the task being performed was a fruitless struggle up a mountain. They enjoyed serving us, and they were given tips accordingly.

CHAPTER 3

OUR INITIAL ROUND OF DISCUSSIONS

After breakfast I called my daughter, and soon the full group was gathered in a large living room overlooking St. Charles Street. Outside the window an historic streetcar went by; not unusual, one went by each 15 minutes. Fred and his brother Bob, a law partner who specialized in automobile accident cases, served as hosts, working the coffee and snack trays out of the kitchen. The group also included other members of the firm: civil attorney Tom Hardcastle, a Berkeley law graduate, Paul Lawrence, a specialist in medical malpractice and a Michigan law graduate; John Hall, who handles criminal cases, a University of Mississippi Law School graduate. Also attending the retreat were the office manager, Mary Holmes, and paralegal, Michael "Rashid" Russell, who was also a part-time law student.

Eddie Bauschard had been confining his New Orleans law practice to criminal defense matters, although he had also been a civil case attorney. Fred had also invited two friends from his younger days growing-up in a midwestern college town. Larry Bach, a high school classmate, was now a dentist with his own practice in Springfield, and Roger Lowe, an older neighbor, was a businessman who had had a clothing store on Central Avenue in Collegeville.

After many hearty handshakes and laughs about getting out the beer, something we vowed to avoid until the evening hours, we worked on setting our agenda and putting forth some goals for the four days we would be in New Orleans.

Fred had clued me in on my role. He wanted me to go through a customer service model I and a colleague used in a book we wrote for the casino industry. But when he indicated that I was now front and center and should begin talking, he added a cryptic remark that "Walker and Hardcastle really doesn't have anything to learn in this area, as we offer the best customer service of any law firm in Las Vegas." I gulped, took a deep breath, and thought, "challenge!"

I felt that I had to draw any problems to be discussed from the group, but I decided to just go slow and let the others join in the talk from the beginning. They rambled somewhat, but they put some good information on the table.

I then congratulated Fred's staff on their success. I indicated that the success had to have had been generated by offering good service. I told them I wanted to highlight some areas that probably contributed to the success so that they would reinforce their good attributes. I thought to myself, this is being "diplomatic." **Good customer service is never a goal reached, it is always a journey that must continue.**

I presented the notion of the service cycle and the concept of "moments of truth." These ideas had been developed by Jan Carlzon when he was the executive at Scandinavian Airlines. In customer service training sessions, I ask members of groups to identify each step of their relationship with a customer—times when they share a human interaction or engender a human response from the customer. The "moments of truth" are special among these interactions as they lead customers to conclude that they either want to repeat the cycle or they never want to do business with the concern again.

I also suggested that we talk about motivation in the work place. I commented that they should share their source of motivation. After all, they were taking time away from their families—at least their evenings and weekend, to be with here for this retreat. They had to be motivated.

Michael gave a sigh, and said, "Look, I love this job and the opportunity Fred has given me, but I'm here out of a sense of obligation and survival. Frankly, I don't know how long I am going to last. Each day I go to the office, the work is mounting higher and higher, and then the weekend comes, and except for holidays and semester breaks, I have 10 hours of law classes. And for these classes I'm also expected to study. I've done this for two years, and if I want to be a lawyer, I am staring at two more years of this. It sure can get me down. Sometimes I wonder if I can last."

Roger indicated that he might know what Michael was feeling. "When I took over my father's store 20 years ago, Central Avenue was thriving with retailers. It was great. We were like a family, we'd have lunch together, and we'd have Christmas parties, and spend a day together decorating the street. Then the mall came, yeah, and the Wal-Mart. We said we'd fight 'em and we did, but slowly our numbers dwindled. I guess the smart ones moved to the mall right away. But we tried everything; special sales, parking tokens, free coffee and donuts, parades, even charity events. But business just kept falling. We ran faster and faster just to stay in place. Nothing ever got any better. Our store was the last clothing store on Central Avenue when we closed it down. I can certainly relate to Michael's frustrations. It was a long haul. I've been there."

Mary offered that her work was the same day after day: greet the clients, open the mail, check the bills, and give them to the financial clerk. Call all the clients and others to remind them of the appointments, or as the need might be to reschedule the appointments. The "same ole, same ole," day after day. But she said that "it never has bothered me—can't really say why, but it hasn't."

Fred said he didn't know what made Mary smile, but it sure helped when the waiting room was packed with anxious clients eager to have major life problems resolved. Mary just smiled, then added, "I don't think I have it too rough. Just think of Shirley—that's Shirley Wicker, our runner—as she drives between the office and the courthouse, to the other law offices throughout the valley, rushing to get papers to them on time, and fighting the awful traffic every day. How she does it, I'll never know. I could never do that."

These were not real answers to the question of what motivated those present at the session, but these were all things we could think about and discuss later. I then decided we could tackle the subject of customer service head-on. I wanted their thoughts about the steps in the service cycle, and what they considered to be their "moments of truth." I indicated that the customer service cycle starts when a potential customer or client decides to go to a particular business, for instance, to a particular lawyer. Then he or she journeys to the office and enters the door. The cycle includes negotiating traffic and parking.

Larry, the dentist, related that he had major problems when he started his business as a solo professional. He was just out of dental school, and he was deeply in debt. He chose the city of Springfield because its ratio of dentists was low, but he could only afford an office in an old house many blocks off of the main street. At first he thought his only advantage was free street parking, but as luck would have it, the parking meters came in during his first year. The advantage quickly became item one on his list of customer service challenges.

Tom sympathized. He too had to work off major college debts when he opened his practice. But just finding clients was his first challenge. He had worked in Las Vegas for a major trial firm, and he had to agree not to take any of the clients of the firm with him when he left. He said at first it was like the proverbial novice stockbroker who was given a phone book and told, "Here it is, your key to success—start calling." As if he was going down the alphabet, Tom just started going to any event where he could meet people. He began shaking hands like he was a candidate for elective office. He even came to think of church as a place where potential clients came to pray. He added that he likes to go to church a lot better now as he has gotten over that phase of starting his business life.

Paul interjected that they were talking about the stage of the service cycle when the client would come into the front office door. He wondered how clients they felt squeezing into a small lobby, sitting on folding chairs where their knees often would bump one another. He offered that the clients must be tense, as Mary had said. Paul said he felt tense too when the clients would come into his office for their initial consultation. Each client seemed to be a brand new case situation, and it was always back to the beginning with everyone, and then step-by-step climbing a hill, wondering if they have a case, and then, what are the damages? Where are the witnesses? Is the client believable? After this, the lawyer has to gather the evidence. This may involve finding a doctor's report, a police report, calling Shirley and asking her to run here and run there, and then, wondering if the client will be there for the next appointment. And after that client, there is always another client.

John said, "Oh, Yeah, and maybe that next client will be the 'client from hell.' You can never tell at first." I asked, "Who is this, this 'client from hell'?"

Larry laughed. "We've had bad insurance representations from patients who never brushed their teeth in their lives." He said.

Roger added his, "Oh Yeah, indeed," and told about the "customer" who ties up two clerks trying on everything, then has the tailor check the outfits, then tries on another suit, only to comment, "Oh, maybe not today," as he or she walks out the door. In the meantime his or her kids run through the store tipping over displays and yelling, irritating the "buying" customers. This is the "customer from hell."

Eddie continued the conversation, describing one client from his civil trial days who kept coming up with phantom injuries. One time Eddie was convinced of the story, and did all the background work. The client kept missing appointments, but Eddie persisted. He even got the other side to make an offer, but the offer was not good enough for the "client from hell."

The case eventually got to court. Eddie poured his heart and soul into his opening statement and he meticulously led his client step by step through his "airtight" testimony. When the opposing attorney got his chance at cross-examination, it became clear to Eddie that there were holes in his client's "airtight" case. The opposition's counsel then presented solid evidence that his client was somewhere else at the time of the alleged accident. Eddie's client began to break down, and by the end of his time on the stand, he was a blubbering, crying idiot. He was dismissed from the stand, the judge immediately rendered the verdict, and then he ordered the attorneys for the "client from hell" to pay all court costs.

The "client" had not advanced any money at all to his attorneys, and of course, the client stiffed Eddie on this obligation. The judge also invited Eddie into his chambers where he was given a severe tongue lashing. "You never know, the next client just might be that 'client from hell.'" Eddie said to finish the story.

"Wow!" I exclaimed, "that's a pleasant thought we can carry over for tomorrow's session."

CHAPTER 4

THE AUDUBON ZOO, DRINKS, DINNER, DRINKS, AND "ALL THAT JAZZ"

The group took a rest break, and we shared sandwiches and soft drinks brought in from "Johnny's Po' Boys" on St. Louis Street in the French Quarter. The "Po' Boy" is a New Orleans invention, a filling meal within a small loaf of French bread. The loaf was stuffed with all the classics—there was lean ham, garlic flavored beef, shrimp, rice and red beans. The sandwich is designed to give energy and to save time for the journey through the day. Other classic New Orleans meals would be taken in at a more proper leisurely pace.

The next stop on our journey was the Audubon Zoo, a half-mile south through the famous Audubon Park. Zoos had been established in ancient Egypt as early as 3500 years ago. The classical Greeks also kept collections of animals to be studied by the public. Ours was an entirely recreational trip, but then I thought that perhaps some of the animals could give us some lessons for life. On the other hand, with Mardi Gras approaching, maybe we could offer more of a spectacle for the animals.

We each had our favorite animals. I was partial to the Kangaroos; Michael, of course, liked the giraffes; Fred was partial to the lions; and Roger, true to his Chicago roots, liked the bears. Jennifer was particularly fond of the swimming seals, and Mary just loved the koala bears. All of us enjoyed the primates swinging in their trees, the bald eagle that sat nobly on its perch in silent grandeur, the flamingos each standing balanced on one leg, the camels standing about in groups, and the hippos in their pond.

We didn't exactly know what to think of the snake that swallowed a rabbit whole, but it was fun watching the African elephant, the dingoes running about, the tapir, and the anteater. All the animals gave us pause to think that maybe we were really living in the zoo, and this existence before our eyes was the real world. As we walked out of the zoo, we climbed Monkey Hill, the only hill in New Orleans. Monkey Hill had been constructed so that the children of the Crescent City could know what a hill was, and artificial snow is put on the hill in winter so the children can experience snow sledding. I had a thought, "Wouldn't it be so nice if all our hills and mountains were just put there so we could have fun." We came back to the Mansion d'le Jardin and lounged about for a couple hours before tackling the evening's "chore."

That evening's agenda started with cocktails at the Columns, a St. Charles Garden District establishment build in 1883. It had been featured in the movie, "Pretty Baby." It was a bit brisk for sitting on the famous veranda, but we took in the history engulfing us from the walls within. From the Columns we moved to the piece de resistance—the dining tables of Commander's Palace. This Brennan family's restaurant on Washington Avenue, across from the Lafayette Cemetery with its eerie above-the-ground vaults, was a gastronomic adventure par excellent. It was truly a celebration with Creole flavors, not soon forgotten (not yet anyway).

The evening was not complete until we jumped into two taxis and ventured to Pat O'Brien's for the mandatory "Hurricane". By the end of two rounds of drinks we broke up and headed home. Well some of us in the group did. I heard the next morning that Michael, Fred, and John had closed down Tipitanas Jazz night club on Tchoupitoulas and Napoleon Streets at 3 am.

On Bourbon Street

CHAPTER 5

AN INTRODUCTION TO SISYPHUS, OUR MAIN CHARACTER

Don't mess with success. If it works best, don't change it. That's the way those of us that got eight hours sleep felt any way. We headed back to the Bluebird Cafe. At ten a.m. we were all gathered once again at the Mansion d'le Jardin for another round of discussion.

I reflected aloud about what had gone on during the previous day. I tried to make sense out of the many thoughts the group had shared. I had participated in a short course on mythology at the University of Missouri, and a notion kept turning over and over in my mind as I heard the comments from the group. I felt compelled to share a story with the group.

Many of their problems and concerns appeared to be the proverbial ones of hitting your head against a concrete wall repeatedly. While some may suggest it is a pleasant exercise— you feel so much better when you quit—it proves to be a really fruitless exercise.

More to point, many of the group appeared to be playing the role of the mythical Sisyphus—pushing rocks up a mountain only to have the rocks fall back to the ground before they could be pushed over the top. Indeed, I felt that Sisyphus could serve as the point of reference for addressing their many problems. The trials of this mythical character named Sisyphus could offer a framework for analyzing many of the problems of life, and seeking solutions to those problems. I told his story.

Sisyphus, the King of Corinth, has been an enduring character who made his first appearance in the literature of Greek mythology. As he has lasted as a figure demanding our attention for nearly three millennia, and as we may see him in the flesh as we observe our bathroom mirrors each morning, it is a stretch to say that Sisyphus is but a mythological creature. **He is real**. Sisyphus also finds that his name bantered about in latter-day non-fiction as he plays roles in the works of Spenser, Pope, and Camus. He was the subject of a painting by Titian.

Like the modern day Sisyphus we may gaze our eyes upon daily in mirrors, the first Sisyphus described in the ancient classics such as Homer's Odyssey and Iliad, Virgil's Aeneid, Cicero's Tuscan Debates, Horace's Odes and Satires II, Ovid's Fasti and Metamorphoses, and Sophocles' Ajax was a sinner. Hopefully, the depth of his sinning has not been visited upon our own personal characters, but there is no doubt, he was a bad one.

Moreover, Sisyphus had a healthy and vigorous disrespect for authority. The name "Sisyphus" as translated from its Greek form is thought to mean either "the very wise," or "a goat skin."

A goat skin was used as a rain-charm, and Sisyphus for quite some time enjoyed a charmed life—that is a charmed mortal life. He was a bad kid who always got away with it.

Those describing Sisyphus have not been kind with the labels they have put upon his head. He was called super smart, cunning, clever, but inevitably the labels were given with a negative connotation. He was also called the craftiest of mortals, and shrewd, as well as a trickster, deceitful, and a man of avarice. Additionally, he was labeled as wily, vindictive, treacherous, and wicked, mean, and a master thief, and a cheater. In some regards, the adjectives have been cast upon him because of the prominence of his adversaries, but then his story also suggests the lack of kindness he gave to strangers and to ordinary people.

The most disturbing portrayal of his activities finds him murdering travellers and taking their possessions. Travellers had to cross the waters from Delphi to the Peloponnesian Islands going by the mountain above Corinth. Sisyphus is seen throwing rocks upon them from the mountainside near their passageway. The seduction of young women was also within his modus operandi.

Sisyphus was the son of Aeolus and Enarete, the King and Queen of Thessaly. He had a strain of the mischievous in his lineage as his great great grandfather was Prometheus, also a well known trickster. His grandfather was Hellen. Sisyphus had seven brothers and five sisters.

Sisyphus married Merope Pleiades, the daughter of Atlas. They had four sons Halmus, Ornytion, Thersander, and Glaucus, who succeeded him as King of Corinth. Glaucus fathered Bellerophon who rode the winged-horse Pegasus across the skies performing heroic deeds while incurring the wrath of Zeus, a family trait by that time. Zeus poisoned the horse who then threw Bellerophon to his death. Sisyphus was also the likely sire of Odysseus another clever wheeler-dealer.

Sisyphus is said to have founded the city of Corinth. Alternatively, it is suggested that he merely inherited the mantle of leadership of Corinth, and that the position of King was given to him by the evil sorcerer Medeia who had ruled since the death of childless King Corinthus. Sisyphus built Corinth into an entrepreneurial center for trade and navigation. He was also a cattleman who took pride in his stock holdings. One of the few decent things he is recognized for is the founding of the Isthmian games. The games were established in honor of his nephew Ylelicertes who's drowned corpse was brought ashore to Corinth on the back of a dolphin. The games became one of the four national festivals along with the Olympic games.

The seamy side of the life of Sisyphus was built upon his dysfunctional family. One of his brothers, Salmoneus, was considered insane. He was hated by the gods and by Sisyphus. Salmoneus had tried to imitate Zeus by using a torch to resemble the lightening strikes of the chief of the gods. With such fakery, Salmoneus was able to seize the control of his father's crown and rule Thessaly. Sisyphus sought the advice of the Delphic Oracle as to how he might destroy his brother. He was told that he must seduce his brother's daughter Tyro. Deed done, this union produced twin sons who were murdered by their horrified mother when she heard of the Delphic bargain. Sisyphus was able to follow through on his plan however, as he convinced the people of Thessaly that Salmoneus was the incestuous father of the slain children. They drove their king out of the town, and

Zeus then destroyed Thessaly with his own bolt of lightening.

The weak structure of the family was also reflected by the incestuous mating of one of Sisyphus' brothers and one of his sisters. Their offspring was thrown to ravenous dogs. Sisyphus also seemed to live on the wrong side of the tracks, at least judging by one neighbor, Autolyces. Like Sisyphus, he too was a cunning thief—in fact, he was considered the greatest thief of all time. He had learned from his father Hermes the secret of changing the form of stolen goods so that they could not be recognized and recovered by their rightful owner. Using this god-given talent (Hermes was the god of cunning), Autolycus was quite successful in stealing many cattle from Sisyphus.

Sisyphus had his suspicions, but proof was not in his hands. That is, not until he branded the hoofs of each of his bulls and cows. Their markings in the mud led Sisyphus directly to the culprit. He retrieved his stock, but he felt it necessary to place a measure of punishment upon Autolycus. As it was his nature, he seized and seduced Autolycus' daughter Anticleia, who was betrothed to Laertes. After he left Anticleia, she married Laertes and bore a son named Odysseus. Lo and behold, Odysseus was a classic liar and trickster. Just like his grandfather and great grandfather—maybe like his father too. Laertes was passive and retreated from an opportunity to hold the crown of Ithaca. Instead he tilled the soil of his estate as a farmer. If character has a place on the genetic chain, it is very likely that Sisyphus was the father of Odysseus.

Sisyphus fate was sealed, however, not from his misdeeds regarding the smaller figures of mythology, but from the tricks he played on the "Big Gods." Zeus was the chief of the gods. He was the brother of Hades who oversaw the underworld, and Poseidon, the god of the seas. Zeus was the father of Hermes and many other of the gods. Zeus was a the ultimate dispenser of good and evil, but he certainly did not possess the purity of a Platonic philosopher-king. His libido would make any male American politician proud. If it wore a skirt, it caught his eye. Especially eye-catching was the nymph Aegina, daughter of the river-god Asopus. Zeus took the form of an eagle and swept down upon her and carried her off to an isolated island.

Sisyphus managed to be wherever he saw advantage, and he was placed where he observed the abduction. Soon he was visited by Asopus who was in a quandary trying to find his precious daughter. Sisyphus had by now built his city, Corinth, and he was saddened by the knowledge that his city lacked a steady supply of fresh water. He declined to discuss the whereabouts of Aegina, but he hinted that if his city had water, he might be able to recall his recent observance. Asopus placed a spring atop the Acrocorinth, the mountain beside Corinth. Sisyphus was pleased and he fibbed on Zeus, telling Asopus where he could find Aegina.

Zeus was furious—Sisyphus would pay for betraying the chief of the gods. Asopus would pay too, as Zeus promptly killed him with a thunderbolt. Zeus had other plans in store for Sisyphus. Zeus called upon his brother Hades, who dispensed Thanatos, the spirit of death, to the earth to capture Sisyphus. But, as we know, Sisyphus was not stupid—he had crossed Zeus and so he was on the look-out for the god's allies.

When Sisyphus found out that Thanatos was coming, he conceived a plan to outwit the spirit of death. He was able to capture Thanatos and place him in chains.

The story of capturing death and locking him up has been retold over the centuries, along with other characters: a Sicilian innkeeper corked up death in a wine bottle; in Grimm's Tales, Hansel put death up a tree; the contemporary Kurt Vonneagut story "Welcome to the Monkey House" repeats the tale in a future where people live forever. The same scenario is played out in most of the cases. First no one dies. Hades gets no recruits for his work in the underworld, but also heaven is deprived of new angels. On earth, the hope of peace that comes with a natural death is denied. Persons with painful afflictions suffer without relief. In time death's captor, here Sisyphus, realizes that the disruption of the common order cannot persist. In this case, Hades sent Aries (the god of war) to secure the release of Thanatos. Sisyphus acquiesced in permitting Aries to take him and commit him to death and the underworld.

This "first" death of Sisyphus was not a totally voluntary act, as the trickster still had another one up his sleeve. He instructed his wife Merope that when death came she was to throw his body into the gutter of the street. She was not to provide him with the proper ceremonies and rituals of burial along with the burial sacrifices which were required. Hence Aries delivered Sisyphus to Hades and his wife Persephone in rather improper circumstances.

Sisyphus raised the issue of his improper burial. Hades and Persephone were quite angered and agreed with his premise that he should be returned to earth where he could chastise Merope and then receive a proper burial and make the appropriate sacrifices demanded by death. Sisyphus promised to return to the underworld very soon, but then he was a liar and a trickster, wasn't he? He refused to return.

Sisyphus remained on earth enjoying the mortal pleasures of being a king. But he grew very old. Then as with other mortals, he grew tired and he began to feel the infirmities and pains of the years. He looked forward to the rest he could find in death. He died of weakness. Hades sent Hermes to escort him to the underworld, and he offered no resistance, no deceptions, no tricks. He welcomed death. Hades, Zeus, and the other gods were pleased to welcome Sisyphus, but they did not exactly throw out the red carpet. This prodigal son was not to be given the fatted calf.

Thcy were somewhat less than forgiving. They judged him harshly, and they assigned him a place not in the heavenly Elysian Fields, or the Islands of the Blessed. Instead he was confined for an eternity in the darker infernal regions. He was given a task he would have to perform forever—pushing a rock. Why was Sisyphus given this fate? Pick the reason. He sinned and he angered the gods. He seduced Tyro and Aeqina, he betrayed Zeus and tricked Thanatos, and he deceived Hades and Persephone. There were reasons enough.

Was he the only person ever given a hopeless punishment? Look in the mirror and perhaps on some days you will feel that he was not alone. But then, in the underworld he was not totally alone either. Ixion who had attempted to seduce the wife of Zeus was stretched over the spokes of a wheel of fire that spun in the air. Tantalus had stolen a dog belonging to Hermes. He also killed his child and served him as food to the unsuspecting gods. As a punishment he is forever being "tantalized" by residing in a lake which recedes whenever he is thirsty, and living under a branch of grapes that moves out of reach whenever he is hungry. The fifty daughters of Danaus are being punished for killing their fifty suitors. The daughters must fill a bottomless vase by pouring water into it.

CHAPTER 6

THE SOLUTIONS TO OUR SISYPHUS DILEMMAS

SOLUTION I: ACCEPT THE ROCK, ACCEPT THE MOUNTAIN

The group seemed to take to the idea that there was quite a bit of the Sisyphus story in their lives. So I asked, "What should you do about it?" The answers started flowing and everyone threw in his and her thoughts. Jennifer offered the advice that she said she gives students at Loyola. "Just take your assignments and your workload and **do** them. **Do it and see how that works out!**"

I let other comments continue until they seemed to degenerate into many side conversations. I said, "O.K., now let's take these ideas and see if they can be organized into a strategy for action."

We had a flip chart available, so I asked Bob to get out the marking pens—we were going to write some things down. The first step in the strategy involved Jennifer's notion. It was simply a recognition that pushing rocks is a part of life, and that we should accept the premise that we will be doing some rock pushing. Bob wrote: I. Accept the Rock, Accept the Mountain.

The idea was broken down into several tactical approaches.

(1) First, Simply Show Your Stamina and "Take It"

Sisyphus took the punishment that was dished out to him. In the account presented by Albert Camus in The Myth of Sisyphus, Sisyphus is seen as almost happy as he runs down the hill chasing after the rock he will be pushing soon again. I shared a bit of sociology along with the story of a contemporary man who "took it," without complaining.

In our politically correct society, phrases such as "take it like a man," are heard less and less, in public anyway. Yet the words do suggest a sense of virtue in the ability to accept the long uphill nature of tasks given to us by fate. It is noble to accept adversity and the frequent setbacks that come when our rock slips out of our hands and rolls back to the base of the mountain.

In many developing societies with populations fighting against the large rock of poverty, a word is used to describe this "male" virtue. The word is "machismo." It is especially prevalent as a force in the popular cultures of Latin American countries. Webster's New World Dictionary defines "macho" as "strong or assertive masculinity," while Webster's Ninth New Collegiate Dictionary defines "macho" as "aggressively virile," and "machismo" as "a strong sense of masculine pride." In the eyes of other males, the man must attempt to achieve the ideal of maleness by displaying values of fearless courage, and valor, and he must welcome challenges of danger and even death with daring, and a self-possessed calmness called "bravado." The macho is stoic to the point where he is considered not to have respect for human life itself. Positive values of pride, courage, honor, charisma, and loyalty are accompanied with negative values of recklessness and aggressiveness.

In our single parent and dual couple working society, we find women sharing the virtues of machismo as much as males. Mary said a loud "Amen," to that thought as I expressed it to the group. Indeed, when you consider the struggles of women to keep homes together while dealing with male machismo behavior, it is often the case that the real endurance, persistence, and stick-to-it-iveness is more a female trait today. In reality it is a gender free notion.

The boxer, the bullfighter, and the more passive worker who shirks not his duty wears the label. In our recent history, the word in its positive and negative senses has been tied to G. Gordon Liddy. Liddy might also personify another phrase: "If you do the crime, you do the time,"—and don't bitch about it. Liddy was the only Watergate scandal participant who refused to give evidence against his co-conspirators, and the only one to serve out the full punishment placed upon him by the judicial process. He made no plea for mercy or special consideration in exchange for cooperation with prosecutors.

Liddy also saw his rock (not Alcatraz, but Louisburg) as an opportunity to build experiences that led to lucrative post-prison activities as an author, public speaker, and radio show host. He chronicles his "struggle" in an autobiography entitled Will. In the preface, columnist Stewart Alsop writes, "In all secret services, it has to be assumed that any captured agent can in time be broken. But there are a few—a very few—captured agents who remained unbreakable...In the case of (Watergate), the stubbornly silent G. Gordon Liddy seems to be the only operative to fall into this category. In wartime (he) would have been festooned with decorations rather than slapped in jail."

In his ordeal, Liddy proclaimed that "I am not subject to coercion," as he advanced an idea heard before: "We can only imprison ourselves." In other words, "We are doomed on the mountain, only if we let the rock and the mountain defeat us." Liddy writes that "life is a series of hands dealt by God, the Devil, and ourselves. God plays it straight and invites us to do the same. The Devil deals marked cards, cheats, and invites us to play it his way. The game is called choices and you must play. The game is over when God says it is and you die. He decides whether you win or lose. You can quit. It is called suicide. If you do, you lose."

The book of Hebrews (12:1) in the Christian Bible gives us another model to follow as it asks us to "endure trials for the sake of discipline," and to "not abandon the struggle." "Let us run with perseverance the race that is set before us," looking to the example of the one who grew not weary.

We are given our days to live and to push rocks. If it ever feels like you are having a particular tough day, and the day is too rough, just try doing without one.

(2) Recognize That There Can Be Happy Contentment in Doing What is Required

Was Sisyphus Happy? Camus thinks so, for Sisyphus was showing the powers that be (Hades,

Zeus) that he could take whatever they dished out. The existential philosopher perceived a smile on the face of Sisyphus as he raced downward to retrieve the rock for another push. When we take life's storms along with the sunshine, we show our fortitude and our independence. In each day there are opportunities to have simple enjoyments. In fact, the back sliding moments may be events that reoccur only occasionally during a day, and in between the events many better things may be happening.

(3) We Should Know that Pushing a Rock is Something to Do

Our rock-pushing exercise with all its effort does fill what might otherwise be wasted, empty time.

When I was in the service, there were many moments of idleness. You know the military saying, "Hurry up and wait." While one waited, one was quite vulnerable. The posture of standing around in apparent idleness is an invitation to be punished or to be put on some detail: latrine duty, a clean-up detail, mowing the grass, or simply being asked to run personal errands for those with a higher rank. The only defense for a person in such a position is to grab onto a rock. For the Marine recruits of Parris Island it was the pocket-sized Marine Corps Handbook. When idle, a Marine boot should always have it in his hands. The sergeant jumps in front of you and yells (rather loudly), "What are you doing 'Prive'?" The only safe response in such a situation is a very loud, "Studying the Marine Corps Handbook, Sir!" "Carry On," is the command that spells R-E-L-I-E-F.

John offered that in the National Guard it is the same, but troops don't have to stand in idleness, they can sit about wherever they might find a convenient place. However, they had better be doing something. The solution? The troop is advised to always have a piece of steel wool near his hand, and also to have a mess kit or an uncovered metal canteen close by. The sergeant yells (not too loudly, it isn't the Marine Corps), "What are you doing corporal (promotion comes faster in the National Guard)?" The acceptable response, "Cleaning my mess gear." (In the National Guard the word "sir" is reserved for officers). "Carry On," is the invitation to return to idleness—just don't be caught writing letters or reading a non-military book, or simply sitting there. The rock of work becomes a justification for the use of time.

Similarly in civilian life, the rock is a badge of belonging. It does give focus to life, it is a point of reference when one awakes in the morning. It is also a part of our introduction to one another, "What do you do?" "What is your line of work?" It is a subject for endless conversation. Without it, people must resort to mumbling words about the weather, diapers and apple pies, and sports game scores.

By accepting a Sisyphus-like fate, we are staking out a position. By working on even very routine tasks—which seem without end, we know what we must do each day, where we must be each day. We avoid anomie. We play a role in the larger scheme of things. We belong.

If you don't like work, try unemployment.

In early 2001, I was able to spend a week in my hometown near Detroit. Each night I watched the local news on WDIV Channel 4. It was not happy news that week, although I found something incongruent in the messages I was receiving. As an undergraduate I had gone to college in East Lansing and studied social sciences. In my classes the professors talked about the drudgery facing the working man. They lectured endlessly about the inhumane nature of the assembly lines that were an essential part of the laboring system in the automobile factories of the state. The workers struggled with hard physical tasks involving a few simple motions repeated time after time throughout the day, and then repeated again the next day—and the next day, and...The workers never saw the results of their labors, nor could they appreciate those results in the factory atmosphere. In fact, the professors provided an implicit but nevertheless strong pitch for staying in school and being able to avoid having to work in the factories. Indeed factory work had to be rotten work.

The news played the story over and over. Daimler Chrysler was going to permanently lay-off (ergo, fire)

26,000 workers, most of whom were in Detroit factories. Recalling my college classes, I thought I might see some relieved, even happy faces as the news crews went to the factory gates for interviews. There were no happy faces there. All were rather grim. One sad worker after another repeated the same woes to the cameras. "What am I going to do?" "Where will I go each day, this is the only place I have known for the past 23 years?" "How will I exist?" "How will I make ends meet?"

These soon to be laid-off workers were pre-playing future times that would be very stressful for them. Unemployment and even normal retirement without planning for the answers to the questions the workers asked can be very stressful. Studies of stressors and their impacts upon people rank unemployment (fired at work) and retirement high, 8th and 10th on a list of 50 factors. The factors are ranked higher than items such as pregnancy, a new member of family, death of a close friend, beginning or ending school. Doing nothing is a pretty good definition of death. We will have plenty of time to do nothing later.

(4) Our Human Game: We Are Not Alone

We all have rocks. They are in our jobs, but they are in many other facets of our lives as well. We are people and what we do is we push rocks. It is what we are supposed to do. In the movie, "The Crying Game," an old story is told. A frog and a scorpion are on a small island. However, a flood sweeps down a river, and the scorpion cries out to the frog for help. The scorpion cannot swim, and he begs the frog to carry him across the waters to a larger, higher piece of land.

The frog, not exactly a dummy, says "Sure, and then you will probably sting me, and I'll drown, and you'll go with me."

"No I won't, I promise, please give me a ride, please. I promise." Skeptical, the frog exacts the promise again, and finally agrees to give the scorpion a ride across the raging river. Alas half the way across the river, the scorpion stings the frog, and the frog goes into a delirium and begins to sink.

The frog cries out, "But you promised, and now we are both going to die. Why, Why, Why?"

"Why, you ask," says the scorpion. "I am a scorpion, stinging frogs is what we do!" We are human, pushing rocks is what we do.

But we do not push alone. If we look around we can see that we are simply not all by ourselves in our Sisyphus-like struggles. It is not an individual thing. Sisyphus was not the only one in the underworld doing an impossible task. In our own struggles we are quite like the little wave that Morrie Schwartz discussed in his conversations with Mitch Albom. (Tuesday's With Morrie). The wave was happy as could be splashing about the ocean. Then he noticed ahead of him that the waves going to the shore were crashing against the cliffs and breaking up. The little wave suddenly shouts in fright to a bigger wave, "We are all going to die, we are going to die."

"Please, my little friend," said the larger wave, "Do calm down a bit. We are not going to die for we are not just waves, we are part of the ocean, and we shall go on forever."

Indeed, in our struggles, we must recognize that the line of time in which we work carries beyond our lives. Our work is not futile although it may appear to be a Sisyphean task. What we do not complete, the rocks we leave that are not pushed over the hill, may be pushed over the hill later by another person. We are part of a human society that, like the ocean, goes on forever.

(5) Pass it On

Generations came before us, they pushed, they sacrificed—for you and me—they struggled, by their own choice so that our lives would be better. Jennifer agreed that she felt that her role in life was not just a wave, but rather it was part of something bigger. During her junior year in college she had a chance to visit France and some of her (unknown before that time) cousins, Alfred, Matilde, and Christian, who lived in Alsace. They took her to Bouxwiller about 50 miles west of Strasbourg where she saw the house in which her great great grandfather was born. He and his family gave up the house and she kept wondering why. Why would a man and his wife and four young sons travel all across France in a horse-drawn carriage just to get in a crowded boat for a journey of several weeks to America? Why would they then trek off to Pennsylvania and start a new life? She thought that the youngest ones might have found the beginnings of some business prosperity, but the older ones didn't reap many commercial benefits during their lifetimes as a result of the journey. And their grandchildren who seemed to fit into the new community could not even speak their language. Jennifer very thoughtfully, said, "You know? They did it for me. They never pushed the rock over the mountain, but maybe I owe it to them, no not them, but to those who will come after me, to keep pushing."

Eddie Bauschard smiled, and said loudly "Cousin Jennifer, my father's family was from Dossenheim, that's in the same area of Alsace as Bouxwiller, you are my cousin." He explained he used the French pronunciation of their name ("Boochard") in order to fit in with the local Cajun lifestyle. He laughed and said something about being "kissing cousins," but then he turned serious. He said that he was really into the family history thing, and he wanted the group to know that anybody who was anybody was from Alsace. The area was once an independent principality, but over the past three centuries it had been a province bouncing back and forth between French and German control.

Eddie said, "You know Jen, your family must have come over just before Auguste Bertholdi sculptured the Statue of Liberty. He was an Alsatian. So was Albert Sweitzer, talk about a person pushing rocks for others." "Ah but the greatest was selected by Time Magazine as the Man of the Millennium—Johann Gutenberg, the man who gave us the printed book, the man who invented the printing press. If you ain't from Alsace, go hide your face. I rest my case."

"Take it easy there counselor," said Bob, who was of Irish-Italian descent. Bertholdi may have been from Alsace, but the name sounds a little bit Italian to me. Sweitzer deserves praise, and I won't slight Gutenberg, but then he didn't exactly invent anything. He just reassembled things. Why, the Chinese had used wooden blocks in printing a thousand years before Gutenberg. Your Alsatian ancestor only changed the wood to metal. And even before that the Chinese invented paper. Now where would Gutenberg have been if he had to print things onto rocks."

Bob's brother Fred, who was a budding wine connoisseur, added with a bit of Italian pride, "Don't forget the Romans." They invented the wine press, and without that idea Gutenberg would have had to keep his hieroglyphics all to himself."

"Ok, Ok, point made," retorted Eddie, "I'll keep him in my heritage, thank you, but I'll admit that Gutenberg was able to push the rock over the top because he didn't have to start the pushing, others had come before and they did a lot of the pushing."

Mary threw another wet rag at Eddie, who was enjoying the attention, saying "And don't be too sure Gutenberg got it over the top, the Xerox people are coming in next week, and they tell me they have the greatest concept in printing yet to be devised. The pushing never seems to stop." Everyone in the room laughed at the good natured bantering.

And so indeed, we may never see the results of our rock pushing, or we may never perceive the results. Yet accomplishment of our pushing efforts can add immeasurably to the advancement of causes well into the future. Teachers face incredible frustrations in their work. Yet their impacts from persisting in the futility of rock pushing may be felt generations later. American historian and philosopher Henry Adams wrote that "A Teacher affects eternity; he can never tell where his influence stops."

An attitude of acceptance can make a life more pleasant. The story of the two stone makers is illustrative. One complained that he had to work in the cold, carrying heavy loads, hammering with shocks of pain radiating up his arms, and at the end of the day, what did he face? Another day of the "same ole, same ole." The other stone maker was asked what he was doing on his job. He smiled and replied, "I am building a cathedral."

(6) A Chance for Empathy

By looking at others in their struggles (including those who came before us), we can seek to share their load by offering empathy and sympathy. This exercise in reaching out is also what makes us human, in fact, it is the essence of what we call community. What can we do when bad things happen to good people? This is the question Rabbi Harlod S. Kushner addressed in a book written in the 1980s. Not much? Wrong. We can offer a hand, a shoulder, a smile, a tear. We can do so, because figuratively if not literally, we have indeed walked miles in that person's moccasins. We can join in that person's circle of life; we can be part of a community. Our rock pushing can be blended with theirs.

(7) Rocks Allow Us to Enjoy What We Really Enjoy

Bad things happen to good people who love their lives, their families, and their jobs. But then many do not like their jobs, and that presents an ongoing challenge, the challenge of impossible rock pushing. Maybe. Roy Kaplan wrote an interesting book entitled Lottery Winners. In the mid-1970s, he interviewed 100 big lottery winners in five states. Most of the winners quit their jobs. His book suggested that people work for functional reasons—for survival and out of habit, and not because of true satisfaction from their jobs. When the people had a chance to get out of the jobs they did not like, they jumped at the chance. Most of these lottery winners were people of lower income levels and lower educational attainment. They did not have the skills necessary to compete for better jobs.

Robert Presthus presents a comprehensive analysis of "coping" with work in his book The Organizational Society. He saw three types of organizational workers—"upward mobiles" who reasonably aspire to success in their job setting, the "ambivalents" who aspire to such success but are not reasonable as they do not have the tools needed, and the "indifferents" who harbor no such aspirations at all. "Ambivalents" are subject to many frustrations, and they may drift into neuroses. The "indifferents" have very little commitment to or identification with their jobs. They withdraw emotionally from their work setting. In his survey of organizations, Presthus found that 90% of the labor force fit this "Indifferent" pattern. They were equally divided among white collar and blue collar jobs. While they were not necessarily unhappy about their jobs, they were not motivated by work. Like the lottery winners that Kaplan found, these individuals looked at work as a means toward securing income and security, and as a means of supporting leisure.

This functional quality of work provided direction for workers studied by Robert Dubin. Dubin examined our Central Life Interest, in a book of that title. While we spend a "very large continuous" amount of our hours while awake at work, the vast majority of us find our central life interest outside of the work place. Until late in the Industrial Revolution work consumed life, now the focus of life is off the job. A lack of ownership in work, overspecialization, hierarchial control of the work place: all these pull people away from involvement in their jobs. How do they stick to it? How do they cope with the rocks of work on these jobs?

Mary gave us a glimpse of the answers, when she discussed her life situation. When she took a job as a legal office assistant, her family really needed the money. To keep her job, she had to struggle to get kids to school each morning, and she had a neighbor baby-sit them in afternoon. As her husband's career began to mature, the money went into college funds for children, then when the nest was emptied, into the "neat things in life." A new room at the back of the house, and travel—ski trips, cruises, and a trip to Europe five years ago that is still celebrated with pictures in the office and around several rooms of her home. The money has also given Mary the opportunity to participate in church and charity work, where she finds most of her closest circle of friends.

Dubin and Presthus find also that most workers can cope with their rocks by seeking motivations from activities off the job site. The fact that jobs provide the mechanism to allow this outside participation makes them acceptable and makes enduring the rock push much easier. There are benefits in acceptance. We keep our jobs, we stick to the important roles in our lives, we sustain our lives, we support others. We do our duty. We may think that our gold comes with golden handcuffs, but we do get gold. Linus of "Peanuts" comic strip fame was asked why he was always clinging to that blanket?" His response was simple, "It's not my blanket, it's my job."

(8) Some Consolation in Acceptance

Jennifer said she wanted to tell a story about why acceptance can work. She indicated that a job she had as a first-year dorm counselor was really bugging her, as she could not find a moment free. She was a graduate student, having to go to classes, and having to study, but every morning before she could get to class, someone would be knocking at her door, and so it continued until late in the evening. She endured, she did not know how, but she noticed that while the door knocking continued, it no longer bothered her. She quickly responded to the person at the door, and she gave fast answers, having heard almost every type of request she could imagine. They were just repeats. Jennifer also was able to make referrals to others for solutions. She knew where the students had to go for help if she did not have answers. She even left her door open in the evening and students looking in the door could see she was studying, so they were a bit more respectful of her time. She sensed that as time went by she was getting into the routine, into a groove. The rock she was rolling was wearing itself down, and she was gaining strength in the process.

So it is with acceptance.

Acceptance is fostered by three realizations as we push the rock over and over. (1) The rock wears down with friction, becoming smaller each successive push; (2) we wear a path—a groove that makes the journey easier; and (3) we develop muscular strength and technique that all make the pushing exercise easier.

(9) We Realize That the Social Order Requires Acceptance

Theirs not to make reply
Theirs not to reason why
Theirs but to do or die...
So rode the six hundred

(*Alfred Lord Tennyson,
The Charge of the Light Brigade)

If other teachers and I did not show up to teach classes, students would not be able to get degrees and seek their mountains. If Fred, Bob, Eddie and the other lawyers did not go to their offices every day, people with major problems in their lives would not have a source for solutions to the problems. If Jennifer did not stay available in her office at night, students would have greater difficulties coping with a large university bureaucracy. If Larry didn't come into his office along with his dental hygienist, his secretarial staff, and his partners, people would suffer painful tooth problems which would make their mountain climbs much more difficult. If Roger had not sold clothing goods, people could not have increased their quality of life and the value of their holdings. **We get a job, and we do it. That's the way society works.**

Robert Fulghum tells us that "All I Really Need to Know, I Learned in Kindergarten." One of the best lessons that will do us well during our entire life is a kindergarten lesson. We must show up when bell rings and the doors open in the morning, and we must stay until the bell rings in the late afternoon. This lesson learned by the masses, allows a society to be a functional society. Indeed, in the infamous book, <u>The Peter Principle</u>, the authors—Lawrence Peter and Raymond Hull—offer the reason that minions keep their jobs even after they reach their "levels of incompetence": they obey the rules. Rule number one is "show up and work through the day." Rule number two is "obey the rules."

While we will discuss ways of making the journey of life and the struggle against the mountain perhaps a bit easier, maybe even ways to avoid the steep mountains and heavy rocks, we still must realize the necessity to stick with our tasks at hand. This should especially be the case when we have deliberately selected the mountain upon which we walk. A popular folk saying is "Go home with the one that 'brung ya' to the dance."

The case of Las Vegas as a gambling community may be used as an illustration. Seventy years ago, the leaders of the state of Nevada decided that casino gambling would be legal. From that time onward they have supplemented that major policy decision with an attitude and with other policies supporting the decision. The state has often come under attack from federal authorities for activities related to gambling, and additional attacks from moralists have been constant.

Those attacking Nevada and Las Vegas have been able to point out many social maladies—personal desperation, compulsive behaviors, family dysfunctions, criminal activity—that are associated with casino gambling. Yet, the state has realized a phenomenal growth of its casino tourism industry and, as a result, has experienced prosperity for a growing population for seven decades. The state has struck to its climb, to the path and the mountain that it has selected.

In contrast, many other states have seen the positive sides of the Las Vegas experience, and they have also legalized casinos. But many of these jurisdictions endorsed their new policy with great reluctance, and with the promise that the negative sides of Las Vegas life would not be welcome. After casinos open, the state authorities tend to see them, on the one hand, as cash cows for the state treasury, and on other the other hand, as some kinds of institutions of ill repute. They impose higher and higher taxes and they institute severe controls. New Jersey regulators even took it upon themselves to oversee the decor and the colors used for casino interiors. Advertising bans have been common.

The New Orleans casino faced a construction shutdown by the city council for three weeks until the operators could find an plan for dealing with the "refuse" behind horse drawn carts that would bring customers to the casino door. The city wanted a successful casino, but they refused to allow the casino to offer hotel rooms or a sit-down restaurant. The casino opened with a fast food area, but all players who sought to alleviate their hunger with junk food had to stand while they did so.

Another jurisdiction even decided that there could be no gambling on Sundays, even though the legalization of casinos was promoted for tourism. These jurisdictions embraced the mountain of gambling, but they did not love what they embraced. Las Vegas loves its mountain, indeed it not only embraced casino gambling, but it married casino gambling, "For the better or the worse." If we are able to incorporate the same attitude of acceptance of our mountain, our climb will be more tolerable.

Perhaps a recitation of the serenity poem is in order at this point. "...Grant me the serenity to accept the things I cannot change, the courage to change the things I can, and the wisdom to know the difference..." Look at the Clock and be conscious that each second passing is a moment of life. Seek to enjoy it wherever you are.

In universities the professors call the time they must be in class with students their "load." That is, if I must teach students in the classroom for nine hours a week, I say I have a "nine hour 'load'." My profession must reflect on our tasks a bit. Is the time of our lives a "load" or is it a "Joy?"

(10) It is Important to Celebrate the Completion of the day, the Journey we Made, No Matter how High Up the Mountain, No Matter if the Rock Slipped Again—The Day is Life: Celebrate

"At the fit hour, 'tis sweet to unbend." (Horace, Odes, Book XII, "To Virgil.")

So unbend we must. Too often in daily life, ordinary life, we get buried in "To Do" lists, and we spend so much time thinking about what we "should" be doing or what we need to get done, that we fail to take time out to pat ourselves and others on the back, and say "Great job, good effort!"

After accomplishing an even small goal, or just trying to push at that rock on the mountain, we must take time out to celebrate.

Celebration helps create joy in our lives. It is a way of acknowledging and rewarding ourselves and others for the mental, physical, and emotional time and effort we put forth. Celebration is a form of expressing appreciation, and it is a way of motivating ourselves, and others, to continue to strive for accomplishment in our lives.

As human beings, we all need to feel appreciated. It is so simple to do those "little things" to express our appreciation and gratitude toward others, yet we often fail to go out of our way to do them. Ultimately it is these "little things" that can significantly impact a person's experience, whether in the work place or at home. When we feel appreciated, supported, and encouraged, we are more willing to go that extra mile and more determined to get that rock moving. We are also more willing to take risks, rather than choosing to stay stuck, or just running downhill after the rock that keeps slipping away from us.

Celebration is an essential piece of the effort to solve Sisyphus dilemmas. It is simple, and it can come in many forms. It can be a little card to say "Thank you," a nice dinner out, flowers, tickets to the movies or the symphony, a facial or massage. It may be giving yourself permission to sleep in one morning without setting the alarm—but not a work day. On the other hand, if a vacation day has been earned, maybe skip a work day.

Celebration is infectious, and the more that it becomes a part of your life, the happier your life will be, the easier the pushing will become. **Celebrate!**

Our trip to the zoo had provided examples of celebration. The sea lions stood out for their exuberance attitudes. Here there were five beautiful water mammals in two connected pools. They had no place to swim but in circles, yet they swam, and swam and swam. As they moved from pool to pool they leaped in excitement and faced the crowds along the fence. They truly seemed to be smiling. It was a beautiful day. They could look forward to a meal at the end of the day and a time of rest. They were happy, and they were celebrating.

As it was approaching one in the afternoon, the stomachs were turning. Fred had some more "Po Boys" brought in for the lawyers and law firm associates as they separated off for a session of their own. Eddie, Larry, Roger, Jennifer, and I jumped on a street car and headed out to Carrollton. Another New Orleans pleasure trove awaited—the Camellia Grill.

Here in an antique-looking corner shopping strip was the walk-in restaurant—just twenty-nine stools. They were arranged around a lunch counter right out of the 1940s (at least one of us could remember the forties). As we looked over the menus, Jennifer said "Put those down, I've been told about this place, we have to have the 'Cannibal Special.'" Eddie grinned, hardly containing laughter. On faith we ordered this unique item, uncooked (I was hoping this was not for serious, but I think it was) hamburger and egg with chopped onion on rye bread. (Talk about a "celebration.") Whatever, it tasted all right to my hungry lips, especially washed down with a coffee freeze and ice cream.

Like the Bluebird Cafe, the service made the Camellia Grill extra special. Waiters in white waist coats and bow ties moved quickly about as if on roller skates, talking loudly and laughing every moment. They engaged each person coming in the door with conversation about sports teams ("How bout dem Tigers"), about party time comin' with the Mardi Gras, about the weather, and asking "Is this your first time at the Camellia Grill, Well we goin' sure make sure it ain't you last time at the Camellia Grill." I wasn't too sure I'd order another "Cannibal Special," but I was sure, I'd be back—someday.

By the time we got back to the Mansion d'le Jardin, the lawyers were finishing up their session, and after a coffee break, I started again with the journey of Sisyphus. Bob got out the flip charts and we summarized the ideas about **accepting the rock and accepting the mountain**.

Table 1. ACCEPT THE ROCK—ACCEPT THE MOUNTAIN

1. Show your STAMINA, show that you can take it.
2. Find a happy CONTENTMENT in doing what is required.
3. Recognize that rock pushing helps you OCCUPY what would otherwise be EMPTY TIME. It is something to do.
4. Know that you are NOT ALONE in the human game of pushing and climbing.
5. Pass it on. Know that your struggles PERSIST BEYOND GENERATIONS.
6. Know that your struggles make you PART OF HUMANITY and help you have EMPATHY for the human condition.
7. Realize that rock pushing enables you to GAIN other things you enjoy.
8. A consolation in acceptance is that persistent rock pushing makes our task EASIER, as the ROCK GETS SMALLER, the PATHWAY SMOOTHER, and our STAMINA GREATER.
9. Understand that unless we all push, SOCIETY cannot SURVIVE. It is a rule of the social order.
10. And CELEBRATE the completion of each day's rock pushing.

SOLUTION II: ADJUST TO THE ROCK, ADJUST TO THE MOUNTAIN

Bob flipped over to some fresh paper, took up the marker, and asked, "O.k., what should we put on the board now?"

John said that he agreed that "We have to just 'take it' a lot of the time, but can't we do something besides just 'taking it'? Can't we make some adjustments?"

I responded, "O.K. Bob? You heard that, write it down— **Adjust**."

I put it back in John's corner. It is a heavy rock. I asked, "What might you suggest?"

(1) Seek Togetherness

John told that while I was gone, they mutually went through a list of concerns for their law firm. He emphasized that we were in New Orleans because we were a team. Parenthetically he asked, "Isn't the rock pushing easier when we work together?"

"Sounds good to me," I offered, "Let's look at the notion of two or more people shouldering the rock on the journey up the mountain."

I discussed Rabbi Kushner's book, When Bad Things Happen to Good People. The religious scholar and popular writer suggests that the journey is bearable, because we are in it together. We can sympathize and love one another while we each face difficult tasks in life. We offer sympathy, we accept it as part of our life adjustment to rock pushing. "Life's a b—, and then you die..." Not necessarily so. With a mutually felt sympathy, life need not be "a b—." And it truly goes beyond mere sympathy too, it involves offering a hand to our fellow rock pusher for the performance of the task being faced. Two (or three, or more) can push a rock easier than one.

When we offer help, and two do the pushing instead of one, we can experience an effect that is called synergy. Synergy or Synergism can be described as "combined action" and "working cooperation" in conditions (according to Webster's New World Dictionary) "such that the total effect is greater than the sum of the individual effects." This was dramatically demonstrated when Adam Smith reorganized a pin making enterprise. There were ten workers each individually making pins. Together they made fewer than 100 pins a day. Each would take a long strip of metal, measure it, cut off a small length, measure it again, roll it several times, and spend time filing down a point. They would return to a pile of metal, and cut a small piece out and then round it. Then they would place the two pieces of metal together and hold them over a fire until the fused. Then they would cool the fused piece, and file it some more. Birth of a pin. Smith reorganized the workers into a single assembly line, and assigned each a task that would have a minimum number of movements. When each was done with his task, he would move the parts of the future pin on to the next worker. In one day the ten workers made four thousand pins.

Roger said, "Oh, that is the old one-and-one equals four trick." He went to a closest and found several metal coat hangers, and he began to unbend them. He re-bent two each into the shape of a triangle. He said, "One-and-One." Then he twisted each side of each triangle outward. "Now he said, let's add them together." He placed them together so that they formed a four-sided pyramid (three sides and a base).

"Hey," said Jennifer, "One and One really equals four."

"Ah, more than that," said Roger, "One triangle plus one triangle equals four triangles PLUS a pyramid!"

Bob jumped into the conversation and told how law case work can get really stressful and difficult. This being the situation, he offered that it is beneficial to bring other partners into cases at various stages of the work, as was the case with a difficult law suit he recently litigated. Bob continued, "Everyone might think that going to trial is a wonderful event. It is not. I can tell you from experience that prior to getting into the courtroom doors, a lot of work has to be done. Forget about the obvious, such as taking depositions, interrogatories, exhibits, and so forth. I'm referring to subpoenas to the many witnesses that must be served."

He added, as well, that if your client or key witness fails to show up, your case might end up being dismissed. Bob indicated that before the court session begins, they must have a set of questions complete and ready to address to the potential jury members. "There are also the arguments you make to the judge regarding exhibits that have been prepared. Will he stipulate that they are good evidence, or will you have to wait until the trial begins, always wondering if a particular piece of evidence will be thrown out of the case? There are also a lot of items regarding the approaches to be taken with potential witnesses, and indeed your own client and the opposite party."

Bob indicated that the practice of law has many different facets, and some lawyers enjoy certain aspects, but they find others tedious and uninviting. Some lawyers love the litigation process, while others prefer to do research, write motions and file papers. In their firm, Bob spoke on, "Fred does the talking in the court room. I do the pre-trial preparation work. Actually, Fred doesn't even look into the situation until there is a firm trial date." This arrangement parallels the traditional British legal division of work between solicitors (pre-trial attorneys) and barristers (court room attorneys).

The firm's para-legal, Michael Russell, makes sure that all the witnesses are scheduled properly, that the subpoenas are properly filed by the court, and crucially, that the witnesses show up in court at the right time. Mary, the office manager, calls all the clients of the firm who had prior appointments during the trial time, and she makes sure they understand the firm's responsibilities. She reschedules their appointments. A crucial part of this process is making sure that these existing and potential clients realize that when their matter gets to court for resolution, it too will receive the top priority from members of the firm.

Partnering and teamwork is synergy. One and one equals four. Or Four PLUS! But here like in Adam Smith's pin factory, the work of four as a team comes to equal the results of the labor of a dozen or more operating as individuals.

(2) Prepare and Use Good Equipment

Larry spoke up saying, "Look it is more than just teamwork. There is also preparation and preparation means having the right equipment if you can get it. We need the right tools."

"Amen," piped in Eddie. "If I was going up a mountain, I would want some good shoes, probably shoes with cleats so I could dig into the pathway."

In an organizational sense, there are physical tools like computers and libraries, but there is a personal tool as well—preparation. Baseball Hall of Famer Roger Maris once said, "You hit more home runs not by chance but by preparation." (Quoted in Thriving, by Edward Zorensky.) Be ready for the journey by having the best training you can get, by using state of the art techniques and devices, by studying the trail, and by toning up your muscles.

Each job requires certain tools, and there is great frustration among those trying to accomplish the job without the tools. Robert Presthus' category of "ambivalents" is illustrative. These include those in the work place who truly wish to advance their career within an organization but lack the tools necessary for promotion. Perhaps the worker doesn't have the necessary credentials, the union card, the college degree. Perhaps the worker does not have the skills required, that is the craft skills or the social skills. The rock slipping is not "enjoyed" by these workers, as each slippage is a great moment of defeat. Like the "incompetents" of The Peter Principle, these workers are most subject to hypochondria as well as genuine physical maladies. Lawrence J. Peter did write a sequel, actually a dozen or so, as it appeared that sequel writing became Peter's "level of incompetence." The second book, The Peter Prescription, lays down an essential plan for success that is based upon being prepared for your job when you take it.

(3) Use Switchbacks and Conserve Energy

Mary offered that the pace of one's work is very important too. "We know that in our day that a 'crunch time' will come. We should not be exhausted when the critical moment comes."

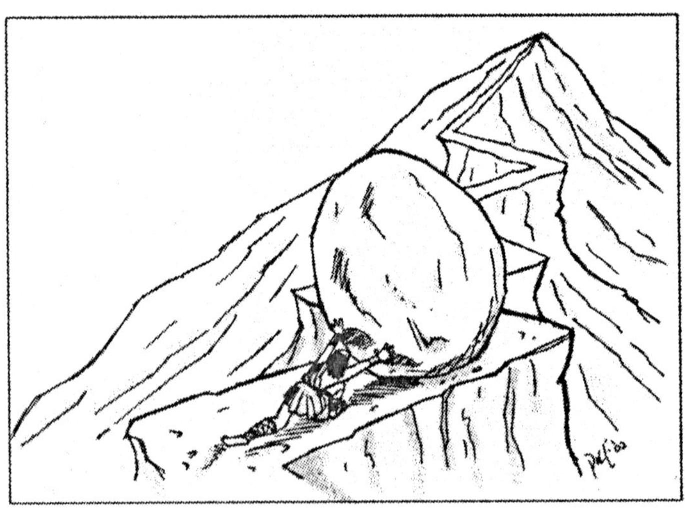

"Oh, Yes!" echoed Bob, "We have our 'Showtime.' Summation to the jury. Boy, you had better be fresh and at your best during summation."

However, the entire mountain slope may looks steep, so how can you be fresh for the last push toward the peak? I asked the group.

Jennifer was a jogger and recreational mountain hiker. She said with a popular collegiate colloquialism, "Well, DAH! Haven't you heard of switchbacks. I've never been on a mountain trail that went straight up a mountain. They always go back and forth with slow switching inclines. For sure, the stretch to the top is harder. It is usually steeper, and that is where the altitude gets you. The air is thinner. But switchbacks allow you to save your energy."

Roger indicated that some of the animals of the zoo provide good examples of how to conserve energy. He said the obvious one is the camel and his hump. The hump is a storage area for fats, which can provide energy for long desert walks where there may be no vegetation to eat. The camel also has thick eyelids that give it shade, and also keep blowing sand from destroying its vision. As well, the camel doesn't sweat, allowing the animal to hold its water supply longer.

Tom added that he really enjoyed watching the Hippopotamus. He said, "You noticed the Hippo was in the water all the time we were there. It spends its entire day in the water. It is a really heavy animal, but it floats, and so its legs do not have to work as much during the day. It saves its energy so that it can come out in the cooler night air and then expend its energy searching for food and grazing. It eats 130 pounds of food each evening."

I asked Bob to write it down. "Use Switchbacks, Preserve Your energy for the Peak Time." Maybe with a burst of reserve energy we can propel our rock over the top.

(4) Make the Pushing and Climbing into a Game

Tom said, "Maybe it's all just a game, can't we treat it like a game. Games are fun."

I offered, "Bob, write it down. That's something to talk about."

We can indeed make our struggles into a game. Maybe it is like painting the rock in your favorite color and pretending that it is a ball. Often we can "whistle while we work," sometimes we can play a radio or CD player with our favorite songs. Whatever is pleasant can be mixed in with work. Charles Coonradt developed the idea of making the workplace a game center in his book, The Game of Work.

I quit playing golf a long time ago. The frustration of the game was too much. I would make two or three good strokes and have an honest shot at a par or even a birdie, and then overshoot a green or I'd three putt. My good play would instantly be negated by a score of six or seven—double, triple bogey. "This stinks," I told myself. So I quit. Now I think that maybe the game of golf should be more of a game. We should only count our good strokes. In every other game we count good things. In golf we count bad things. Maybe we can count just good things at work too. Don't count the times the rock (or ball) slips down, count how far up the mountain you pushed it this time, how fast you pushed it this time. Go for a personal best.

Mary commented that her financial records clerk, Elizabeth Boatright, had the hardest task in the entire office. Elizabeth had to face a stack of work each day and plough through it, paper by paper, bill by bill, until the stack was done. Always it is the same kind of work, as if she were on an assembly line, no variation.

Bob spoke up. "You know, Mary told me about Elizabeth, and I felt the same, so for a treat I took Elizabeth to the special gourmet room at the country club for lunch, you know the one the casino executives go to each day. I did it for secretaries week, so everyone would understand. I really want to keep her working for us, and I want to know she's happy at work. She began to open up about work, and you know, she loves her work. She shared her secret with me. For 'Liz it is not boring work. She told me "no way."

"Elizabeth has a scheme. Most days she simply goes through the stack of papers. But about once a week she takes a two to three hour break, either mid-day or in the late afternoon. During this time she reads about her hobby. You notice her books about gardening and the pictures of flowers on her wall, or she e-mails letters to her friends. This breaks up her work routine, but it also forces her to change her pace. On those days, she also takes out a stop watch and she sees how fast she can mow down the stack, focusing her concentration of energy. She also monitors her efforts by recording the last time that a paper had been returned to her for a correction. She celebrates whenever her streak of days without a return, or a mistake, becomes a personal best. She also celebrates when a record streak ends. Her personal best is now 63 days, and she is working on a 24 day streak of mistake free days, that is days since she was asked by someone else to make a correction. I can tell you that the temporary we had during Elizabeth's vacation last summer made over a dozen mistakes in a two week period of time. My friend Sandy Mitchell over at O'Leary and Lawder says that their record clerk can't go a day without at least one mistake. Elizabeth says it's a game, and she loves games. She looks forward to her play day each week."

Bob broke in and recalled that he had had a similar conversation with their runner Shirley Wicker. He said Shirley enjoys a challenge she has placed upon her self. She is careful never to get a traffic violation, but she calculates the shortest route to each assignment, and she times the traffic lights, and seeks to reach a destination with the fewest red lights. She also keeps a records of smiles she receives at the offices to which she delivers papers. She's conscious of initiating a smile and seeking to find out the names of the people in the offices where she goes. Shirley tries to use a name in a greeting at each office. Just before we left for New Orleans, I asked her how things were going, and she said it had been 17 days since she made a delivery where she didn't get at least one smile back. She had gone a month without using the wrong name for a person she greeted—that is in an office she has visited before. Funny, she said it was a game too."

(5) Visualization

Part of successful game playing involves visualization and imaging. John indicated that one thing that helped him in particularly troublesome criminal cases was developing a focused image of a jury returning a verdict in his favor. He imagined the bodies and faces of jurors walking out of the jury room, then they stand in their box and take their seats. The foreman rises as the judge address him saying, "Have you reached the verdict?"

The foreman responds positively and then states, "We have found for the Defendant." John consciously thinks through the scenario as he wakes up and as he goes to bed during the time of the trial. Having the focus gives him an extra drive toward a successful resolution of the struggle.

John's experience is not unusual. It is called visualization. It is used by many successful people in various human endeavors. Let me mention a few stories that are illustrative.

Jerry Lynch and Chungliang Al Huang tell one story in their book Working Out, Working Within. In ancient China an accomplished musician participated in an unsuccessful political uprising. He was arrested and kept in solitary confinement for eight years. He was then rescued as a new regime came to power. Only a few weeks after his release, his friends asked him to perform at a concert. He responded that he was delighted to do so. His musical peers judged that his concert was the best performance they had ever heard on his stringed instrument.

How could he have performed so well on an instrument he had not played for eight years? Actually, he had played the instrument in his mind, and he had postured his hands and arms as if he were playing, and he did so repeatedly everyday. He had heard the sounds as he slid his hands and fingers over the strings. He had imagined his concert after his release and it was the best he had ever given.

In sports psychology the practice of visualization is advocated. Many positive results are presented in stories. One Air Force pilot who had loved playing golf had to eject from his plane over Hanoi. After serving over four years as a prisoner of war and then being released, he was invited to participate in a pro-amateur golf event as a courtesy and honor. He shot an 78, two less than his pre-capture handicap.

"Amazing good luck. Is it beginners luck, or re-entry luck, should I say?" asked one professional player in his foursome.

"Luck, phooey," responded the pilot, "I never three-putted in four years." He had not, nor had he failed to clear a sand trap in a single shot, nor had he missed a green in the regulation two or three strokes. And he had played golf every day, at least thirty-six holes a day for all those years—in his mind.

In 1989, the University of Michigan basketball team suffered some rather embarrassing defeats in the middle of the season. As the league championship began to slip away, their coach, Bill Frieder decided it was time to regroup. He knew these were the best players he had ever coached, but things weren't going well. He gathered the players together and shared a vision and dream with them: a championship beyond the Big Ten league. He placed a poster on a wall in the locker room. It was giant photograph of the N.C.A.A. national basketball championship trophy. He then wrote the name of each remaining team to be played on large pieces of removable tape, and he added six strips of tape representing games in the national tournament. He placed the strips of tape on the poster covering the trophy. He then asked the players to think of the trophy each day. As they played their remaining games he removed the tapes with each victory. The team bought into his vision.

And the vision went beyond the coach. As the season was ending with a new winning streak for his team, the coach was offered a job at Arizona State University and the offer required an immediate response. Frieder accepted the offer, but as a result of the acceptance, he was immediately fired as the coach of the Michigan team just as the team was offered a spot in the national tournament.

The new coach, Frieder's assistant Steve Fisher, had never been a head coach before. As he greeted the team as their new coach, he took them to poster showing one half of the trophy. He asked the players to keep a vision of the entire trophy firmly in their minds. They did, and six victories later they were the national champions.

In an experiment, two groups of young athletes were asked to prepare for a basketball-shooting contest. One group practiced free throws by taking fifty shots a day for two weeks. The other group, which knew about shooting foul shots, was asked to spend the same amount of time visualizing taking the shots. In the contest, the visualizing group made seven percent more successful free throws.

Lynch and Huang write that, visualization is "a planned, conscious use of the 'mind's eye' during a deep, relaxed state to create desirable and fulfilling images of a similar future event." The process functions by "cueing the body to synchronize millions of neural and muscular activities in a dress rehearsal of future events," during which the person draws upon as many of the five senses as possible to "formulate clear vivid images." In so doing, "the pictures developed will be more easily interpreted by the central nervous system 'as if' they were real."

We all have talents, but more is usually necessary for us to get what we desire in life. We need a motivational drive that may be encompassed in dreams and fantasies. The conscious dream gives us direction, and like the concept of "anticipatory socialization," it can get us "over the rainbow." Robert Merton conceived this idea, suggesting that in large organizations, the ambitious, "upward mobile" workers would not look to their peer group for role models to emulate, but rather would look to people in higher levels of the organization. They would imitate the behaviors of their superiors in styles of clothing, speech patters, and recreational habits. When persons were to be selected for promotion, the superiors would look at these workers as ones who would "belong" in higher level jobs. Moreover, after they received promotions, they would more quickly adapt to new social relationships than would workers who had not engaged in "anticipatory socialization."

(6) Daydreaming

Complimenting and perhaps at the same time contradicting the notions of visualization and imaging is the concept of daydreaming. Imaging is a specific focused kind of daydreaming. Both are very conscious activities. Daydreaming encompasses a more generalized use of imagination. In contrast to sleep-state or sub-conscious dreams, daydreaming is for the most part controlled activity, and is also considered to be positive in substance.

To a considerable extent it is an activity of healthy well-adjusted persons. It is a coping mechanism for dealing with many of the absurdities of life, including the type of Sisyphean absurdity we may confront in the work place or any other place. Scholars who have considered the subject have even developed a Daydreaming Scale. People who measure high on the scale exhibit lower heart rates even under stress. Their bodies have less reaction to stress in other ways too. Daydreaming is also associated with lower levels of aggressive feelings.

Not only can daydreaming help a person adjust and cope with seemingly endless tasks, by enhancing patience, but it can also help the person take other positive steps toward fulfillment of tasks in front of them. Daydreaming awakens the creative (right) side of the brain and may thereby be especially useful in decision making situations. It can help a person work out new pathways to goals that are considered desirable. It is a way of release and healing for bad feelings toward one's environment. It is also a vehicle for improving interpersonal relations. Persons high on the Daydreaming Scale have more positive and friendly social encounters. Daydreaming can also help improve the memory processes. Children are encouraged to use fantasy and daydreams in play, because they present an opportunity for growth. And even as mature adults, we are not too old for growth.

The conscious side of daydreams allows us to call up pictures of a positive past or an enjoyable present unlike sleep dreams, which quite often tend to be negative replays of recent activities.

Larry interjected that he daydreams several times each day, in fact he feels that it is more refreshing to have five or six one minute daydreams than to have a fifteen minute break. He likes to let his mind wander to good times he had in school, to old friends, and to the time he got the top score among all the students of his class on an examination. He said his recent daydreams drifted back to a party over the holidays. He said that after his daydreams he was energized to say, "Now open your mouth wide."

Daydreams become dysfunctional only when they are excessive and when conscious efforts to control their occurrence at inappropriate times (or for great lengths of time) fail.

(7) Enjoy The View Where You Are—Smell the Roses

Jennifer suggested that the mid-day can be more pleasant with daydreaming too, actually with moments of reflection that are different from daydreams. She said that maybe wc should take a moment in the middle of our day and just ponder where we are in the scheme of things and appreciate good things. "I guess it is like daydreaming, but you know on my mountain hikes, I like to stop and enjoy the view, even if I don't get to the top of the mountain. Even if I turn back and say enough of this mountain for today."

John agreed, he said that he likes to go out to Mount Charleston on weekends. He said, "I cannot agree more, the view can be great, even if it is only one-half-way up the mountain. I have climbed Mt.Charleston (11,900 feet) many times, but only once have I made it to the summit—Charleston Peak, three other times I have made it to the 11,000 foot plateau. I have walked up the mountain a dozen other times. Every time I have marvelled and rejoiced at the magnificent views that have been given to me by the Creator of the Mountain. You don't have to be at the peak to enjoy the beautiful views."

(8) Take Vacations

Besides taking moments to ponder and to smell the roses, we can use moments to refresh our spirits and our energy supply in other ways. We can take vacations. We can occasionally take refreshing vacations far away from the work place for weeks at a time. But each day we can take vacations at our work place as well. And they really do not have to last more than a minute or so. I described a one-minute vacation to the group.

A one-minute vacation is a very conscious use of mind for escaping from the drudgery of tasks without end. How can we take such a vacation? Close your eyes, then breathing slowly and deeply, count downward from ten to one, pausing between each number. As you do this imagine going downward on an elevator. Repeat this exercise three times, and then imagine the elevator doors opening. In front of you is the most beautiful sight you have ever seen, or ever dreamed of seeing. You have just taken a one-minute vacation.

Paul said it works with isometric exercises as well. He offered a couple of exercises that can be done at a desk or in a confined space. Each exercise can also be done within a one minute time period. In one exercise, Paul told us to push our hands together and increase the amount of pushing pressure until the muscles shake. "Keep pushing for ten seconds. Then ungrasp your hands and hold them outward, again imagine a pleasant thought as you sense the relaxation with energy escaping through your fingers. Do this three times." In a second exercise, you rub your hands together faster and faster until they become so hot they burn. "Then hold your hands out and feel the tingle as you relax thinking nice thoughts. Repeat this exercise three times as well."

We all took a real deep breath. I said, "Ah! Very soon we shall celebrate."

(9) Find New Opportunities on the Hard Mountain Trails

The cliche is "make lemonade when you are given lemons." The task is simply to keep your eyes open to new possibilities as you are pushing the rock up the mountain.

Tom related that he was leaving town driving on I-15 toward Mesquite for a golf date at the Casablanca Resort when a Las Vegas Metropolitan Police officer flashed the dreaded red spinners and motioned him over. Tom said he talked to the policeman, and "I guess he was having a slow day, cause he seemed to just want to talk. I had been doing 78 in the 65 zone, so I was his guest." Tom went on, "So I asked him about life, and he poured it out a bit, saying he likes it but his family worries about him too much, always thinking the big 'What if?'"

Tom probed a bit and found that the officer had not planned at all for "What if..." Tom continued, "I assured him that all people, even those in boring 'safe jobs' should do some planning. I said, 'look, I'm paying this ticket,' (it was no big deal as the officer said since it was under 80, I get no points for the violation). I said 'if you drop by tomorrow, I'll structure a will and a plan for you at no cost.' The next day the conversation continued, the will was written, but I also had an invitation to speak to the police union, and now I provide any policeman with a will at no cost—and no obligation. Really, no obligation. On the other hand, I do seem have several police officers giving me client referrals with civil cases. They don't do criminal referrals. That wouldn't be right, and we don't go out and directly solicit those kinds of cases anyway. John's criminal work is mostly a service for our other clients. It also allows those clients to refer friends to a lawyer they know."

A potentially bad experience was an opportunity. A $75 dollar fine, and it led to cases worth 1000 times that much (or more) to the firm.

At this stage Paul spoke up. He offered his words in a very serious tone. As he spoke slowly he commanded the undivided attention of all of us. He mentioned that he was hesitant in sharing his story, but he felt that it really fit into the particular moment. He hadn't told his colleagues about this before. He had been given a very big rock, and he was able to convert it into an opportunity. He continued, "It was a Saturday morning, August 9th, to be precise. It was two weeks before I was to start my first year of law classes in Ann Arbor. I was with a group of my friends. All of us had recently graduated from the University of Iowa, and we were at Lost Lake, Minnesota, where Peter, a classmate, had a family cottage. My friends were getting ready to go into town, when they yelled for me to wake up. In a moment of silly exuberance, I impulsively jumped out of bed, and ran out of the cottage door. I continued to run across the lawn and out onto the pier. I dove off the end. They day before, I had also dived off the pier, but this time I dove downward instead of outward. My head hit a rock and my neck cracked. I was unconscious. Fortunately, Peter observed me as my body was in a dead man's float. He pulled me from the water. Paramedics were working me over when I awoke. I was paralyzed from the neck downward."

"Needless to say, I had to take a 'medical redshirt year' from law classes. Instead, I spent two months in a St. Paul hospital where doctors did a spinal fusion. They took part of my hip bone and inserted it into my neck. While during the initial stages of my ordeal it appeared that I might never walk again, I was able to walk out of the St. Paul hospital with the help of crutches. Six months of rigorous occupational and physical therapy followed."

"I had always wanted to be a civil attorney. However, as a result of my many many contacts with the doctors and nurses, and my very personal and intensive interest in the procedures they used, I decided that I was going to specialize in medical law."

"I had a head start on other attorneys in this specialty when my practice began, as I not only was familiar with terminology and procedures, I was also able to better empathize and sympathize with clients who had suffered major injuries in accidents that may have been caused by careless actions of others." A nearly fatal tragedy has turned into a lifelong career opportunity.

Bob took out his marker and wrote: "Seize the opportunity presented by the mountain."

(10) Celebrate Each Victory

We were approaching the end of the afternoon and the sky was losing its red and orange luster. Night time was coming. Now it was fun time. We celebrated the day with a cab ride to the French Quarter and a dinner at the Court of Two Sisters on Royal Street. As I took in the libations and the Oysters Rockefeller (an invention of Antoine's just over on St. Louis Street), I wondered just who these "two sisters" might be. Perhaps they were hostesses, special entertainers for the festive crowds. But alas I found that they were long departed. Their building had actually been constructed in 1822, and it was their dry goods store. The highest and best use for the site was undoubtedly its current use.

The "meal" of enjoyment continued after dinner as we strolled to Preservation Hall next to Pat O'Briens on St Peter Street. This cultural icon of the French Quarter has been cooking music since the twenties. Not just any music—authentic jazz. The landmark facility serves no drinks or food. We just sat on grungy hard wooden benches. Well, Mary and Jennifer preferred the cushions on the concrete floor. Rustic, but wonderful. The music held us captive for over two hours.

With the music still ringing in our ears, we still had one obligatory task yet to do. The Cafe du Monde beckoned with the smell of chicory-flavored coffees (they had decaf alternatives as well), and their famous beignets—deep fried sugar powered invitations to a coronary embolism on the spot. We survived, found two cabs and arrived safely back in the Garden District. There in the drawing room was Bob's chart listing the lessons of the day.

Table 2. ADJUST TO THE ROCK—ADJUST TO THE MOUNTAIN

1. Seek TOGETHERNESS and an extra hand to LIGHTEN the LOAD.
2. PREPARE and use good equipment, such as cleats on your shoes.
3. Use SWITCHBACKS and CONSERVE ENERGY for the thin air and steepness of your final steps on the mountain.
4. Make a GAME out of your rock pushing journey.
5. VISUALIZE the good things at the end of the journey.
6. Take time to DAYDREAM.
7. ENJOY the VIEW and SMELL THE ROSES during your journey up the mountain.
8. Have a VACATION during the journey.
9. SEEK out OPPORTUNITIES in the obstacles on your pathway.
10. CELEBRATE the steps up the mountain, your personal bests, and each of your victories big and small.

SOLUTION III: RESTRUCTURE THE SITUATION

According to the plan Fred made for securing the Mansion d'le Jardin, we were served a full course breakfast on that third morning. We started with full fruit plates of fresh Hawaiian pineapple, mangos, and grapefruits along with juices. This was followed by lavish plates of eggs benedict with Canadian bacon, fried Cajun blackened pan fish, and artichoke bottoms. Of course, it was all accompanied by an endless flow of Cafe au Laits.

We walked the extra calories off with a quick stroll around Audubon Place and through the park.

When we re-gathered in the living room to start again, it was 10:30. Before I could try to call the group to order—they didn't provide me with a gavel—Paul was shouting out, "Hey is it all about us? Is this just an attitude adjustment retreat? Can't we do something to make the situation itself a better one?"

Bob agreed. He said, "Look, I am writing down 'Restructure the Situation.' Now let's have some ideas."

I said, "Paul?"

He responded, "You bet, I'd get a hammer and smash that rock up into small pieces, then I'd take them up the mountain and throw it over."

"Good thought, let's see if we can run with it."

(1) Break the Rock Up into Smaller Pieces

We reflected that Michael faced a two-year uphill struggle toward finishing a law degree program. The struggle was to be shared with his family. Two years—

forty weekends a year, then another twelve weeks of studying for the bar examination.

That is a pretty big rock. However, his struggle would be more manageable if he could somehow break up the big rock into some smaller stones.

There is a story of an old grandfather clock. He stood proudly in the drawing room of a palatial mansion on display for admirers with the best tastes and the deepest pockets. One day the grandfather clock noticed that there was a new young grandfather clock across the carpet. He greeted the young clock with a bright smile "Why, Hello, is this your first day here?"

"Yes," answered the young clock, "I'm only one month old. They just brought me from the store. Have you been here long?"

"Why," said the old clock proudly, "I've been here for 90 years, and I have ten years to go."

"Oh, that's a long time."

"Just you wait," said the old clock, "You are going to be here 100 years too."

"Oh, that's exciting. Tell me how many ticks will I have to make in a hundred years?"

The old clock pondered and thought a minute, "A hundred years of ticks?" He replied, "Well, you have sixty ticks a minute, and that is 3600 ticks an hour. In 24 hours that makes 86,400 ticks a day, and with 365 days a year, that makes 31,536,000 ticks a year, but figuring in a leap-year each four years, that averages 31,541,400 ticks a year. And let's see...you have one hundred years, that makes, three billion, one hundred and fifty four million, and one hundred forty thousand ticks." You've done one month, that's 2,592,000, but you've just started, over three billion to go."

The young clock began to sweat and shake, saying "Oh, my God, three billion ticks."

"Yep," said the old clock, "over three billion more ticks."

The young clock shook harder and harder, saying "No, too much, too much," and he crashed over into a big heap of metal parts, dead.

The old clock was a bit startled too. But the next day he noticed that yet another new clock was in the place where the other young clock had stood. The new clock struck up a conversation. And the new clock also asked the old clock how many ticks it would make during its hundred years. The old clock paused and smiled. He said, "just one tick each second."

Michael didn't have to push a two-year rock up a mountain. He just had to go to next weekend's class. And he only had to study one hour at a time.

The rocks we are asked to push are often very large ones. But we can take a hammer, and we can smash them into smaller pieces, and we can carry the pieces up to the top of the mountain one at a time and throw them over to the other side.

When I was in law school, I didn't have the family responsibilities that Michael had. Nonetheless, I felt that it was going to be an endless struggle. There was not a glimmer of light at the end of the tunnel. I had trouble focusing on studies, as I had interrupted a quest for a master's degree by entering law school. I was quite unsure of my goals. Frustrated, I quit, and I returned to finish the master's degree. I later moved on to doctoral studies, realizing that the process would take longer than getting a law degree. But step by step, seven years went by, and I had a doctoral degree.

The doctoral program of study was no easy task, and thoughts of quitting did re-occur, but the capacity to break up the long journey into shorter steps and a persistence in taking the short steps one after another, but one at a time was a winning formula.

Not all Ph.D. students finish. Most that quit the journey, quit at a stage that is called "A.B.D." That means, "All But Dissertation." People that reach this stage are often called "A.B.D.'s." It is no disgrace to be an "A.B.D." Many have very successful careers in life. However, many others struggle with desires to be part of the academic life around major universities. The trouble is they don't have "the union card." They may teach a course here or there, or they may just settle into a teaching position at an institution that takes them away from the mainstream of intellectual life they enjoyed as graduate students.

Why do they quit? The structure of the Ph.D. program is not "finishing" friendly. The student can ease into the program with individual courses, then more courses, and more courses, each requiring some small research project. There is also a research tool requirement that might be satisfied by taking a foreign language examination or statistic courses. When all that is done, there is a big comprehensive examination (or preliminary examination). Generally this exam covers materials from the courses taken.

When the examination is completed, the student is an "A.B.D." The only thing remaining between the student and finishing the Ph.D. program is a massive individual research project, a dissertation. The project must deal with an original research question that has never been explored by anyone before. Advisors can be helpful, or advisors can be bastards ("I went through hell for my Ph.D., you're damn well going to go through the fire too.") But either way it's a big big rock. The rock is even heavier as the slope of the mountain leading to the Ph.D. gets steeper and steeper as the journey progresses. Many quit, but some make it to the top by taking that necessary one, but only one, step at a time.

Michael agreed, adding, "You know, I can also try to not let it come down on me all at once, by just concentrating on what's on the plate not today, but for this meal."

Bob got the marker and wrote:

(2) "Push only one rock at a time—Focus

Over the Christmas break at the end of 2001, I was at home with some friends when the telephone rang. I could not believe it, it was former President Bill Clinton. He addressed me by name and began a conversation about the national Democratic Party. He called me personally! I began to respond, but he just kept talking. Alas, I realized it was a clever recording job. He made his pitch as I invited each in the room to listen in to the call. Just think, former President Clinton is still a viable force for fund raising activities for his party.

We may often break our rocks up into smaller pieces. However, even if we can't always do so, we can make our journey easier if we just make sure we push only one rock at a time. During the latter years of the last millennium, the United States went through a real life soap opera observing the antics and activities of President Clinton. Clinton's family life was lingering on the brink as revelations of his moral lapses were exposed on the nightly news. A personal financial scandal seemed to be mixed in with the stories of his escapades with a young female White House intern.

Congress impeached the president for a litany of wrongs genuine and far-fetched, and he was actually put on trial in the United States Senate. He was not convicted or removed from office, although he lost a major civil law suit and was ordered to make a monumental payment to a woman he had been accused of sexually harassing. Yet, he not only saved his office, but through it all, he was able to perform all his chief executive roles as a foreign policy leader, a leader of a military campaign, the country's domestic policy leader, and as the leader of his political party. Many observers, even some neutral ones, consider that he did a fairly good job in the process. He maintained support for his programs in congress, and he oversaw a sustained period of economic growth in the country. He also led his party to victories in two national elections.

How could he do it? How could he just carry on? The answer: he pushed one rock at a time. He compartmentalized. One day he was a defendant, and he concentrated on defending himself. The next day he entertained a foreign dignitary, and he focused upon foreign policy. One day his marriage seemed to be in a storm, the next day he was helping his wife build her own political career (successfully). Amidst the whirl of turmoil, he remained the most successful find raiser his party ever had. He compartmentalized his concerns, he kept his many rocks separate, and he pushed only one at a time. He was able to push many of them upward on his mountain. He also rejoiced often in celebration. He certainly could celebrate!

Fred suggested that the Clinton story had a predecessor story in 1990. He told about the Running Rebels run to the top. The University of Nevada, Las Vegas Running Rebels of the 1989-1990 season provided another example of winning by pushing only one rock at a time. The basketball team had over time gained a reputation consistent with its name, "Rebels." The coach recruited players off of playgrounds of the inner cities where many of them had not enjoyed the best leadership and supervision during their youth. The National Collegiate Athletic Association (which regulates college sports) constantly had the university under investigation for alleged recruiting violations. The pressures of possible penalties loomed over the 1989-1990 season. Every time the team had a victory and rose in the standings, another potential charge was in the media. Injuries to key players also added to academic ineligibilities and player suspensions for picky items such as not paying hotel phone bills or tardiness in repaying student loans. One player was suspended for ordering a room-service sandwich in a motel after a road game. The coach rarely knew what players would be available for the starting lineup, let alone the bench.

When things finally calmed down and the team was playing well together, the Rebels faced Utah State. After the game, players started shouting at one another and fists started flying. One Rebel player even hit the Utah State coach. All of this was on national television. Fortunately, there were no injuries, but three more Rebel players were suspended for several games. Nevertheless the team was able to win the league tournament and to win a spot in the national tournament.

In the national play-offs (the "Big Dance"), the team performed badly in early games against lesser teams. They were able to come away with some unimpressive wins. Then they started to jell. They began to play together as if they were a fine-tuned machine. All the players were eligible, and they defeated some very good teams. After five victories in a row, they were in the final championship game. They were pitted against Duke, a perennial national powerhouse. The game was a dream game for the

Rebels, everything went right. One of my students was a benchsitter who would be put into games in order for the crowds to cheer the stars as they came out for their final bows. This would only happen in games where the result was already determined. In this championship game he was allowed to play for over three minutes, and he actually scored two three-point shots. The Running Rebels emerged with the national title and a thirty-point victory. It was the largest margin of victory ever in the championship game, and the Running Rebels of 1989-1990 were the only team ever to score over 100 points in the championship game.

The coach was asked, "Amidst all the turmoil this year, how did you do it?" His answer was simple, "Focus, we kept basketball on our minds, all the time. Only basketball." And they just played them "One game at a time."

Unfortunately, a championship does not always complete the job of pushing rocks over the peak. A championship, a victory, must be sealed with a celebration. The basketball coach and the university president had been in a bitter struggle with one another. The struggle eventually resulted in both individuals leaving the university in semi-disgrace. The president went center stage after the victory and proclaimed that "UNLV is a great academic institution." Quite a non-sequitur given the situation. The university never put up a sign proclaiming to the world that the team was the national champion. (Any Iowa farm town will put a sign at the town limits proclaiming that its girls high school softball team won the regional finals in 1983). Even the fans refused to reflect on the victory, instead their rally cry immediately became, "Repeat." They couldn't understand that the rock pushing was done for the season.

Well, the team tried, but an N.C.A.A. basketball championship is quite a heavy rock, and the next year the Rebels lost a very close semi-final game to the focused (on revenge?) Duke team. Since 1992, the Running Rebels have not gone beyond the first round of the national tournament. It just seems that there are no more celebrations around the campus.

Fred offered that the fall of the basketball fortunes at U.N.L.V. was really quite dramatic. "Too bad there wasn't a way to stop the rock on its downward course."

Bob said, "The basketball program should have had some sort of fall back position, maybe like digging a pit to trap the rock as it fell."

(3) Dig a Pit so that the Falling Rock Doesn't go all the Way to the Bottom of the Mountain

A pit can consist of any measure the organization can embrace to preserve the level of success made on previous journeys.

Paul was unsure what the basketball team could have done, but suggested that the law firm's manual of standards served as such a pit. He commented that when he first came to the firm, the clients would walk in the door, and they were haphazardly assigned to whomever was available at the moment. Each lawyer had his own way of talking to new clients, and rarely did they write down their procedures. Indeed, they didn't follow the same procedures each time.

Tom pondered the fact that they all seemed to be reinventing the wheel with each client, and that there had to be a better way. He instructed each lawyer to compile notes on each new client. He collected these after a month, and he discovered that the firm could be much more effective in its use of time if it followed some basic patterns with each new client. Michael was given the responsibility of developing a questionnaire that could be given orally to the clients while they were waiting to see a lawyer. As a result, the clients could be funneled to specific attorneys who specialized in particular kinds of cases, although all the attorneys had experience in the full range of civil cases handled by the firm. Criminal cases, however, were directed to John who concentrated on these matters. By screening clients, time was not wasted by lawyers shuffling clients this way and that.

Besides procedures, Fred said that the firm's manual addressed sources of information, the names of doctors and other experts that could be called into action on their behalf. The manual also presented all the forms that might be encountered in litigation matters with comments on essential factors that had to be included along with time requirements for the forms. Information was also included on computer usage. While many of the items would be useful for attorneys anywhere, much of the information was specific for use in the firm. For instance, a computerized file on each client was started when the client first came in the door. For any future matter involving that client, the file could tell the attorney about the client's history.

I put my professor hat on and suggested that the notion of utilizing routines is basic for organizations. The effective routine is a pit that can keep the organization from falling back to the starting point after each situation is handled.

Sociologist Harold Garfinkle writes that the use of "Routine (is) a necessary condition of rational action...This ability depends upon a person being able to take for granted, to take under trust, a vast array of features of the social order."

Public Administration scholar Ira Sharkansky wrote a book (The Routines of Politics) about the use of routines in public decision making. Without routines—such as a reliance upon the figures in last year's budget in planning next year's budget, borrowing ideas from similar organizations and governments, assuming that similar sets of facts lead to similar conclusions— politicians would never have time to go out and shake hands and collect campaign contributions.

Max Weber, the father of sociology, found that rational bureaucracies expend substantial amounts of energy collecting information and keeping records of cases. We all benefit by taking stock of what has been, and either formally or informally measuring effects and results.

(4) Use Pulleys, Levers, and Fulcrums

The journey up the mountain is impeded if those for whom you are making the hike are throwing extra weight on top of the rocks, or if they are above you pushing downward on the rock. But if as in a sense of teamwork, they are also helping, it can be like a lever of extra strength. For instance, clients can be detectives and help gather all the relevant information needed to prove a case. They can buy into your task and commit to show up for all appointments on time. They can help clear the pathway, and they can even be pulleys helping you lift the rock.

Larry found another lever that made his relationships with his dental patients much better. He made their struggles a bit more convenient, and for him his efforts became like a pulley. As we related earlier, the dentist had located on a side street thinking that ease of parking would give him a start-up advantage in his new practice. But alas, the city put parking meters on his street in the first year he was located in his office. What could he do? Larry did not wait to hear the anticipated complaints. When a patient checked in with his receptionist, the patient was immediately asked if he or she was parking at a meter. If the patient was, the receptionist took down the car's location and description, as well as the time and how much time was on the meter—according to the patient. Larry kept a drawer full of change, and he had the receptionist (or at busy times an extra office assistant) feed the meters. The patients were also informed to bring any overtime parking ticket right back to the office as soon as it was received. Larry paid the tickets. (If they were paid within 24 hours the fine was only five dollars). This was a wonderful lever or pulley, and it established an extra measure of goodwill with patients, and he felt that it led to many referrals.

(5) Use a Back Ramp

A back ramp can help propel a falling rock back up the mountain. When the rock rolls down, it keeps rolling up the back ramp, then down and up the mountain again, rather than resting at the base of the mountain. The standards book can be a pit, but it can also be considered a back ramp that helps keep a falling rock from staying at the bottom of the hill. So too can a good customer service system.

In any organizational endeavor involving interactions with people, good relationships for the future can be quite helpful. By doing the job well one time, you can build for repeat interactions that can be successful. How you left the rock on the last journey becomes very important. In the examples from the arena of customer service, we may think in terms of paying clients. However, that would be limiting our perspectives quite a bit. In most organizations there are myriad other customers around you each day, and they are not just those who bring financial rewards to the organization. Anyone who can help you deliver in your task for the organization should be considered a customer. So what can you do to make your customers wish to return to help you on your next journey up the mountain? You can leave them happy. Not always possible—this is true. But find out.

Follow-up on your journey, was your effort one that satisfied the co-worker, the supplier, or the paying client? If it did, make sure you let them know it was gratifying to be able to work with them and serve them. Make sure you let them know that if any problems arise out of the experience, you are available to try to make it right. So when indeed things don't go right, you do make it right.

In customer service studies it has been found that it is so much more expensive to win a new client than to keep an old client. Roger piped into the discussion, agreeing. "Oh yes, it is ten times as costly to get a new customer into the door. And guess what?" He added, "That new customer has absolutely no loyalties to you. Indeed, by his quitting his last service provider, he is suggesting he is not a loyal customer at all. Do one little thing wrong, and all the advertising and good will needed to get him in the door is right out the window. My repeat customer, that is the one I want to keep. He's loyal."

It is important, he related, to make sure that the loyal customer—actually all customers—leave with good feelings. The moment of leaving the store, or the job, whatever, is a definite "Moment of Truth" on the service cycle. The last impression is a very strong one. This is why you must confirm with the customer that the moment was a good moment, and if it was not, make it a good one if you possibly can.

"It's a funny thing, Roger added, "but when you make a mistake or sell a faulty product, it is an opportunity to grow." "By going the extra step to make it right, maybe discounting a replacement item, or throwing in a few pairs of socks or a tie, or making sure you personally deliver a replacement item to the customer's home with an apology, the customer remembers. He remembers that you know you are human (just like he is), and that you can make a mistake, but if you do, you feel bad about it, and you treasure his future business."

Roger told of attending a marketing seminar given by the Nordstrom's company. They relish in correcting mistakes—not so much that they make them on purpose. But in over-correcting for bad customer experiences, they have created legends about their service quality. These legendary stories are spread by word of mouth, and like a back ramp at the bottom of the mountain, they help propel the falling rock right back up the hill after it hits bottom.

Roger said other aspects of customer service were like pulleys and levers helping his attempts to climb the mountain. It is important to get the client on your side pushing with you—that's a lever each time. He offered that the Louisiana Cajun custom of always giving a little bit extra with each purchase is critical to success. "They call the little extra 'lagniappe,' and it can be a free calendar, a comb, match book, or an extra item if they purchased a dozen of something, but it is always a bit extra that confirms to the customer that he or she received a bargain."

(6) Blast a Tunnel Through the Mountain

There are several notions that can constitute radically different thinking that can help you get to the other side of the mountain without having to go over the top directly. You can blast a tunnel though the obstacle in several ways: perhaps you can out-source some of your workload, develop a new communications system, or find a new computer program.

Fred found a tunnel to new clients. His major concern during his first year on his own was how to get clients without having to engage in very expensive advertising. The need for marketing for new clients is as old as business itself. Fred related, "When I joined my fraternity in college, I could not believe how much time we would spend on rushing new pledges and making sure we had plenty of members. The idea is that you always want to keep the organization alive and well."

Fred had been working for another law firm and periodically employees would bring their traffic tickets or friend's tickets to Fred and he would take them to court with other matters. Fred did not mind at all, because doing one ticket or twenty tickets was roughly the same, and he had to be in court anyway. The experience was in the back of his mind when he ventured off to start his own firm with Tom. They soon hired Elizabeth for the staff. Elizabeth's husband was a taxi driver, and he had had several moving violations. For taxi drivers tickets are not a small matter as points can lead to suspensions of driving privileges, and this means that their livelihood is challenged. But when Elizabeth's husband had Fred's help, Fred could assure him that the charges would be reduced and no points assessed unless the violation was particularly serious.

Fred didn't mind handling the tickets as a favor to Elizabeth's husband, but one day the taxi driver asked him to handle tickets for taxi driver friends of his. He implied that Fred should do it at no cost. The request seemed to Fred to be a bit audacious—asking for help for people Fred did not even know. But Fred is a natural politician, he just smiled. His first inclination was to jokingly laugh off the request pretending it wasn't serious. But he paused, and then a light clicked in his brain. "Oh, Yes! Yes!" He thought, and soon he was saying it out loud. "YES!"

The taxi driver repeated the request, and he asked if it would be a "problem." Now Fred had his strategy in mind. "No! No! No! No problem." Problem, hell. This was a "godsend." Fred said "tell your taxi driver friends to come to me with any moving violation ticket, and I will handle for free, and tell them in no uncertain terms that there is absolutely NO obligation on their part. It is a free service." At first it was word of mouth, but within the week Fred formalized the offer, and he had a brochure printed and distributed to all taxi drivers. In Las Vegas they constitute a tight-knit fraternity of over 2000 drivers.

All of the taxi drivers are potential civil clients. All of them have friends that are potential civil clients. And each of them goes by an accident scene every day, and probably stops at such a scene every week or so. Fred was really helping this group of connected citizens, and they responded. Soon he had lines of people waiting at his doors when he opened certain mornings.

True to his word, there is no obligation for the service. He does keep his brochures (the taxi brochure and the general firm brochure) handy and available for all that come by the office. He also keeps a large stock of business cards on tables in each corner of every room of his office complex. The printed materials seem to say "take me." And the stock has to be replenished frequently. The service has certainly paid off in terms of getting new clients and good clients. It has also provided a measure of good will reflected in an improved image in at least one corner of the legal profession in Las Vegas.

Sometimes the mountain comes to you. Whether there is a concerted conscious effort, or it is just plain luck, the mountain is there. And if one keeps his or her eyes open, it can happen just as quickly, a tunnel can be blasted through the mountain.

(7) Blast the Top Off of the Mountain

Fred found a tunnel through a mountain with his program for taxi drivers. Paul offered that the firm could also blast the top off of the mountain. When he said that, a few in the room laughed, but all looked at him with puzzlement. He was undeterred by the skepticism. He said that the first words his torts law professor had said in his first day of law school was still in his mind. The professor said, "You never lose what you settle."

Michael wasn't attending the University of Michigan Law School. He said, "What do you mean, I've never heard that, please explain."

Paul went on to elaborate. Paul had had a great medical malpractice case where his client had been in a coma for 60 days. The client survived and was able to recover to a major degree, but the client had not fully recovered, and some damage was going to linger for a long time. Paul had believed from the start that the doctor had administered the incorrect dosage of a drug, and that that had led to the damaging coma. In fact, in the course of his investigation, Paul was able to get the doctor to admit that he had over prescribed the medication. Paul filed a law suit asking for a large sum of money damages.

While the two sides were engaged in the evidence discovery process before the trial was to begin, Paul learned something that the other side did not know. Paul's client had a history of abusing illegal narcotics. Only Paul knew. Yet he strongly suspected if this matter went to court, the other side would find out one way or another about his client's drug habit.

The other side approached Paul with a settlement offer. It was generous, but not nearly the amount requested in the suit. Paul had a very blunt discussion with his client in which he suggested that the illicit drug habit was probably unrelated to the coma, but that the evidence, if exposed, could be quite damaging in front of the wrong jury. The client was disposed to go along with Paul's advice. Paul then made a reasonable counter offer. The Doctor's lawyers, and especially his malpractice insurance company, eagerly jumped at the chance to settle. They were quite happy not to have to face a jury with this case. So was Paul.

There are many wonderful things about settlements in legal disputes. They save time. They save considerable expense. They avoid all anxieties and doubts about results, and they help the parties get on with life. Best of all, settlements are final. They cannot be appealed. It is like blasting the top off of the mountain. Michael got the point.

In the academic profession we often blast off the top of mountains with our research projects. While we all seek to write the great academic book, few of us actually do. Yet if we don't, the research projects we start need not be dumped as more rocks thrown to the bottom of the mountain side. A book not finished can always be an article in a major academic journal, or maybe an article in a minor academic journal. If we can't push it that far, it can always be a paper given at a major academic conference, or, O.K., a minor academic conference.

(8) Gather Up Your Faith—The Mustard Seed Can Move the Mountain—Excavate the Mountain

Roger faced the same mountain with a heavy rock to push for many many years. His clothing store was on a downhill slide, and he tried everything, pulleys, levers, teamwork, and excavations, but he just couldn't make it go. He refused to get off the mountain, yet he was wearing down. Early retirement was not at all appealing to him. He never kept his eyes off the mountain peak. One day a glimmer of sunshine broke over the peak and shined down on him. It beckoned him to another mountain. All it said was turn around, it is right beside you.

Central Avenue in Collegeville had become "yuppyfied" and "boutiqued." Roger was in Chicago for a reunion with his St. Rita's high school classmates. They attended a White Sox game, and afterwards a group drove to Rush Street for some night life entertainment.

Chicago is many things. One of the things it is is an Irish City. Roger and his buddies wandered into an Irish Pub. While the spirit and spirits overtook him he found himself in a booth with the owner of the pub. Roger kept saying, "Man, this is the place for Central Avenue. Don't you want to expand? Man, this is a place for Central Avenue." And so the plan began to unfold.

The pub owner indeed was thinking about being in college towns. Roger was losing money running a clothing store on Central Avenue, but his building could be housing a winner, an Irish pub. Roger didn't own his building, but he had a five-year lease with three years to go, and he had an option for five more years.

Roger engineered the deal. The owner of his building was approached by the pub owner. The owner was happy to let Roger make the sublease, and he agreed to assist in the necessary remodeling efforts. The Pub owner was willing to pay three times what Roger was paying for the lease, he even gave Roger an equity share in the business in exchange for consulting services in developing the local market. Roger can now approach his retirement years at the peak of his earning power. Roger found another path that took him around his mountain. Indeed, he excavated the mountain out of site. He celebrates because his rock is on the other side of where the mountain had been.

(9) Go Around the Mountain

We can also go around the mountains. We can search for the gap. We can see opportunities to do things differently. Yesterdays pathways need not be the ones we take tomorrow. In businesses we can always be building bridges to others and trying new things. We can use consultants, use different fee arrangement, non-contingent contracts, agree to the number of hours we will work on the case at the start, request pay in advance from clients who might just be those "clients from hell."

There is a wonderful story about the newly married housewife who baked a ham for dinner. Prior to placing the meat in the baking pan, the wife cut a fairly healthy sized portion off of the ham and threw the extra meat in the garbage. Much of the extra meat was very good meat. After watching his wife do this on several occasions, her husband made the inquiry as to why she was throwing good meat away. She said that she was a good cook and the results were good. He agreed with her on that, but still thought it was strange. She added that they both knew her mother was a wonderful cook, and she learned this manner of cooking from her mother. He had the good sense to just be quiet on the matter.

However, a week later when the wife received a phone call from her mother, the wife thought she should bring the matter up. The mother knew exactly what she was talking about. The wife asked, "Why did you throw part of the ham in the garbage when you cooked it?"

Her mother started laughing. "Well, don't you know how in that house we lived in the kitchen was so small, and we didn't have room, let alone money to have more pots and pans. The pan was simply too small to hold a full ham. It was simply easier than buying a new pan."

If we accept every mountain as it is, we may neglect to see that there is an easy path that will get us to the other side without a lot of heavy uphill pushing.

(10) As You Make the Adjustments, Do Not Fail to Celebrate

When you make progress, and can say, "I tried and I accomplished," you have to Celebrate. Celebrate your progress, no matter how far the journey took you. The journey is a victory.

CELEBRATE!!!

Our third day session ended in the mid-afternoon, as we had planned a quick trip to the World War Two Museum. There we got a good appreciation for the rocks others—those of the "Greatest Generation"—had pushed up mountains so that we could be here freely planning and discussing our career development. That generation of our parents and grandparents had a major mountain to climb, and they climbed the mountain and pushed the rock over the top. While their accomplishments must always be celebrated, they serve also as an example for the accomplishments that our generation and the next generation will be called upon to complete. And these too shall be celebrated.

The next stop was the faculty lounge at Tulane for the pre-game buffet. We then witnessed the Green Wave basketball team take on the mighty Cardinals of Louisville. Unlike U.N.L.V., the Tulane team had never won the national basketball title. However, you could not tell it by the crowd. There was an excitement in the air as the game began. While it was unlikely the team would be invited to a post-season national tournament, the fans responded to each good play—a good pass, a blocked shot, a rebound, and of course, a basket—with wild cheers.

When Tulane rallied at the end of the first half and went into the locker room with a three-point lead, you might have thought it was a championship game. A standing ovation was followed by the pep band playing the fight song three times in a row. All during half time the place was a-buzz. The enthusiasm lasted until the closing minutes of the game even though the home team fell behind by ten points and struggled to keep the loss margin down to a respectable six points. Forget the championship, I craved that excitement for U.N.L.V. again.

For some of us the game was followed by a trip to the casino. But Saturday was going to be a special day and a long day, so even those of us that ventured to Harrah's Jazzville Casino did not linger long playing blackjack beside the statue of Louis Armstrong.

The next morning we had rolls and coffee for a fast breakfast, and then we headed out to the Oak Alley Plantation. Before we left the Mansion, we read the words on Bob's chart from the day before.

Table 3. RESTRUCTURE THE SITUATION

1. BREAK the rocks into SMALL PIECES
2. Push ONLY ONE ROCK at a time.
3. DIG A PIT for backsliding rocks.
4. Use PULLEYS, LEVERS and FULCRUMS.
5. BUILD A BACK RAMP so that the energy of the falling rock helps it back up the mountain.
6. BLAST A TUNNEL through the mountain.
7. BLAST OFF the TOP of the mountain.
8. Gather up your Faith. Use your mustard seed, EXCAVATE the Mountain.
9. FIND A GAP. Find another passageway around to the other side of the mountain.
10. CELEBRATE each time you deliver a rock or part of a rock to the other side of the mountain.

The Oak Alley Plantation House was 40 minutes west of New Orleans on the River Road. The road took us alongside the twisting Mississippi and through several small Cajun villages. The house we toured had been built in 1839, but its fame was of a more recent vintage. Ann Rice had used the site as the setting for her novel Interview with a Vampire, and Tom Cruise starred in a movie of that title. Much of the movie was filmed on location at the Plantation.

SOLUTION IV: REASSESS THE JOURNEY

We were back at the Mansion for "Po Boys" by noon, ready for the last session. In final sessions of seminars participants are often asked to reflect and assess the content of the program. But sensing I might try that tact (I really hadn't made such plans), John preempted me. He said, "Look, I think we have to assess this whole Sisyphus thing. We have rocks and mountains, but do we really need them. Let's just reassess whether we could do without our rocks and mountains all together." I agreed that it was an idea worthy of pursuit during our last hours of contemplation.

I asked John if he had a starting place for the conversation. He said, "Sure I do. Why don't we just say 'No' to the rocks and the mountains." Bob wrote "Just Say No" on the flip chart.

(1) Just Say No

Look your mountain over carefully. There are mountains you must climb; there are rocks you may not have that much choice about pushing. But think—"Is this mountain that is in front of you one of them? Is this really 'your' rock?" Maybe you cringe at the thought of the push and the climb, but you are doing it by your choice, and there are other choices. Very possibly there is a choice to say, "No! that is not my mountain, and that is not a rock I am going to push!"

Consider Sisyphus. Maybe he had a choice too, but he accepted his futile fate for reasons alluded to above (he accepted the time for doing the crime, or maybe he wished to show the "big" gods his ability to "take it"). But sometimes, there is no good reason to accept the mountain, and maybe even for Sisyphus these were not good reasons.

Perhaps Sisyphus could have "Just" said "No! I will not push that rock up that mountain!" What would Zeus and Hades been able to do to him? Kill him? Hardly, he was already dead. Make him burn with pain? Hardly, he was already a resident of Hell, and the flames were already raging about him. If we say "No" to a mountain that is destroying our spirit, a rock that might be breaking our bodies, what punishment awaits us? Consider the possibilities of just walking away. Consider when it might be feasible to just walk away.

In our initial session Eddie told us about the "Client from Hell." Roger discussed the "Customer from Hell." What good does it do us pushing rocks up the mountain just because they appear at our door? Think of your experiences and try to perceive the characteristics of these clients and customers, and when people with those characteristics come around your entrance door, be ready to show them your exit door. I asked Tom and Fred if they ever thought about what makes a client from Hell. Tom offered that he had had enough experience with them that he should know them from a hundred yards away.

I asked for an example, and he and Fred just looked at each other, smiled, and said "Joe" at the same time. Tom continued saying that Joe came into his office one day to inquire about an accident he had just had. He was severely injured and felt that he needed an attorney to make sure that the "damned insurance company pays a lot of money." Tom added, "As Joe continued to talk about his injuries, it became abundantly clear that our firm would not be able to satisfy him, because no amount of money would be enough for the injuries he felt he had. Money just can't compensate for some injuries, both physical and emotional. I told him this, but the more I tried to dissuade him and tell him we were not the firm for him, the more Joe was 'chomping at the bit' to have us sign an agreement to handle his case."

"Oh, I could sense trouble, but finally I agreed to handle the case. Then Joe started to call our office every day. I had to tell him that he would not be able to process a claim until his medical treatment was completed and we had the doctor's bills. Then he would call the next day and I'd have to go through the same conversation again. A few weeks later his doctor called and said that Joe was missing his visits for treatments."

Tom continued saying that the doctor said he got calls from Joe too. Joe wanted the doctor to confirm that he came for treatment when he did not. "When I called Joe about this, he stated without missing a breath that he indeed asked the doctor to indicate he made more visits than he really did."

Joe said, "Look you're a lawyer, come on. the more money for me means the more money for you. Don't be kidding me."

"I insisted that he was quite in error, that we did not conduct business this way. Joe's comment was all I needed, as if I did not have reason before. We immediately withdrew from the case, and I told him so in no uncertain terms, indicating that if he continued to call us, we would refer his doctor's statements to the appropriate people, something we probably would never do."

Joe was flabbergasted. "How can you withdraw from a case when you could make so much money?"

It wasn't hard. Indeed it was a relief. In the movie "Wall Street" there is a telling quotation from the actor playing the father of a corporate raider who was selling out the father's firm. "I don't go to bed with no whore, and I don't wake up with no whore. That's how I'm able to sleep at night." Tom added, "It is really best to avoid getting involved with people like Joe in the first place."

"O.K.," I said, "Tell me about how we see Joe coming?"

Tom paused and said, "Bob, get your marker pen out, let's see if we can make a list." Thinking out loud, the lawyers began to list the following characteristics:

1. The "Client from Hell" is always "greedy." Enough is never enough.

2. The greed comes out early in discussions, as the client's focus is almost always on money, not on relieving his injury.
3. The client always is eager to let you know he knows more than you.
4. The "Client from Hell" has a hard time remembering critical details of the incident behind the legal controversy.
5. The "Client from Hell" keeps thinking that someone owes him, but isn't exactly sure who or why.
6. The "Client from Hell" has a history of seeking legal recourse for a wide variety of problems.

Roger indicated that he could probably draw a profile of his "Customer from Hell" also. He added that he wished he had when the store was still open. He indicated he would have politely told the customer that they were busy. If there were no other customers in the store at the time, he would quickly find that the sales people should be working on a survey or on the inventory. "'The customer from Hell' would be a self service customer, and if that meant we lost him to the self-service mall, so much the better."

(2) Choosing the Mountain with Care

It is important to think through whether you have an opportunity to refuse to push rocks up certain mountains after you have tried it repeatedly. It is also important to be selective about the mountains and rocks before you begin your climb the first time. Think through the reasons you are at the base of the mountain ahead of you:

- Is there another mountain that is more appealing where you could make a better climb?
- Are you prepared for this mountain?
- Do you know the pathway?
- Do you like the prospect of climbing with the people who are around you?

You may also address these ideas regarding changing mountains:

- Avoid being stuck on mountains because of foolish choices.
- Check your thoughts. Seriously ask yourself if you are expecting something too good to be true.
- Are you being greedy?
- Do not betray others or become involved in unfair climbing tactics that may put you onto slopes that are difficult to negotiate.

Remember that Sisyphus did not come to his mountain and his rock just by chance—he betrayed the powers that be. He interfered with activity and "pleasures" of Zeus, the most important god. He captured Thanatos, and then he cleverly tricked Hades, and in the process lied to the guardian of the underworld. He earned his mountain by questionable behaviors. Don't repeat his mistakes—if you can avoid doing so.

(3) Find another Mountain—Find Other Rocks

You can find another mountain. At some time you can get another job. You can return to school, develop a specialty, change locations. These are not easy alternatives, but they do exist for most of us. Nevertheless, we should not spend valuable energy we need for pushing our rocks on searching for other activity all of the time, or even much of the time. But then there may come a time...

You Should Be looking for Another Mountain When:

- Time doesn't pass, it just drags.
- You can't celebrate at the end of the day.
- Your moments of happiness are becoming fewer and fewer.
- You do not feel you are needed.
- You think you could be more helpful elsewhere.
- You do not feel you are doing your best.
- You feel unprepared for pushing up the pathway.
- You find it difficult to enjoy the view during the journey.

My day job is as a professor in a graduate studies program in Public Administration. Most of my students have full-time positions with local government agencies (so actually, almost all of my classes are at night). My students are searching for more knowledge and a higher level of skills by returning to school. Well, that's what I always hope. But what I know is that they are seeking to open doors to either promotions within their agencies, or opportunities to move into positions with either another government agency or in another line of work. Some of my students are in other lines of work and wish to position themselves for government work or for other opportunities.

Michael had received a business degree as an undergraduate. As an athlete—he was on one of the UNLV Rebel teams that reached the "Final Four" in the N.C.A.A. basketball tournament—he made many contacts with local business people. In Las Vegas, that quite often means casino executives. As Michael has "presence" (like 6' 10" of "presence"), he was directed toward security work. He accepted a position as an administrator of safety programs for a large casino resort. The job was simply not a match for his aptitudes. Because he had a "people" personality he used new contacts and gained a position in personnel work with another casino. Personnel work is people work? Right? Not! He enjoyed some opportunities to participate as a teacher in training programs, but he found that more and more he was involved in a pile of paperwork and technical rules regarding everything from details of union contracts, equal employment recruitment, tips and overtime, and occupational safety minutia.

He wanted out, but then he also wanted to be directed toward something else. He continued his education with a Masters of Public Administration degree thinking it was appropriate for his organizational work in the resort industry, but at the same time hoping it might lead to something better in the public sector. As he progressed through his courses, he was still unsure.

He then met Fred who had been a basketball fan and also a graduate of the M.P.A. program. Fred and Michael talked for a long time about both their futures. As the local university had just started a law degree program, Fred urged Michael to seek admission. That step was successful, and then Fred persuaded Michael to quit his work with the casino and start working in his law firm.

The work in the law firm would enhance his legal education, and also it would offer a depth of preparation that could confirm Michael's selection of a new pathway that would be the location of his new rock. It has not been easy as we have seen. Indeed, Michael knows well the difficulties of the journey. But he is convinced that he has found a mountain he wants, rocks of his choice.

(4) Don't Push Others' Rocks for Them

I love Kangaroos. That is the main reasons I wanted the group to go to the zoo. I love to see the Kangaroos jump, it's like watching Michael Jordan going for the slam dunk. I really wanted to see the 'roos leap. I got to the fence of the yard which held the kangaroo and some of his other outback mates. Majestically he stood tall. Slowly he turned and looked me right in the eyes. My eyes pleaded and so too did my lips, "Leap, Leap you gorgeous creature." Finally, as I heard my voice becoming audible to those around me, I gave in to my inner urges and I yelled, "Come

On, Jump!" To no avail. The Kangaroo turned the other way to lie down on the grass.

The Kangaroo had to reside in the Audubon Zoo. He had to occupy the yard and be watched by crowds. But he didn't have to jump. Not for me, anyway. He had his rock, the Kangaroo did not have to carry my rock too. They may look you right in the eye too: the people expecting you to do climb their mountain. Just be sure the job they are expecting you to do is the job you want to do, the job you are expected to do. It is always appropriate to help people with their jobs, but don't allow others to dump their rocks on you. Think kangaroo.

(5) Think of Other Pathways and Mountains for the Rock You Must Push

Earlier we mentioned the advantages of settlements in law cases. But those are ad hoc solutions for problems. There are other avenues for conflict resolution that can be regularized as alternative mountains. Private arbitration is now being used by many attorneys, much as it has been used over the years in labor disputes—especially public labor disputes. Universities are turning to alternative scheduling of classes, and especially to long distance learning structures using not only television but the latest computer developments. Technology is going to be holding out the promise of new structural arrangements for much of our work in the future. Hopefully there will always be libraries with books, but the near future promises that most publication may be through electronic means. We need to be ready to recognize easier pathways for our rock pushing chores, the new pathways are coming.

(6) Delegation: Let Others Go—Let Others Grow

During the mid-1980s, I spent a year teaching with the U. S. Air Force in Europe. I taught one semester at Upper Heyford, England. Each night after class, I would drive to my residence in Croughton Village, park, and walk across the yard to the Lion and Eagle Pub. I would ritually pour down a pint or two of Guinness or some locally-brewed beverage. There I met many of the townsfolk. One night I was confronted with some friendly jeers as I came into the Lion and Eagle. "Hey, American! What do you think about your President Reagan now?" Unaware, I asked what they meant. "Why, the B.B.C. News reports that your President Reagan fell asleep during a meeting with the Pope."

"Oh," I responded, "Is that News?" I offered that my President Reagan had fallen asleep a few weeks before during a cabinet meeting. I mentioned that he was an old man and that cabinet meetings could be quite boring.

"Well," one pub regular blasted back, "Our Maggie's not a sleeper, she stays wide awake during cabinet meetings. What do you think about her?"

I replied that Prime Minister Margaret Thatcher was one of my favorite politicians. I indicated that she was one sharp "in-charge woman." I added that she would be in control of any cabinet meeting she attended, and that she could argue on the spot (without cue cards) on any issue, and that she was very very persuasive in promoting her point of view.

"Well, we have one sharp, as you say, 'in-charge woman' as Prime Minister, and you have your President Reagan, who sleeps on the job. What does that tell you about our two countries?"

I paused a moment, trying to decide whether to say anything or not. But then after two "bitters" in me, why would I hold back? "Look," I said, "It appears that you Englishmen just might need leaders. We don't!"

Maybe that's not exactly true, but there is some truth in the statement. The English very often wait for their government to tell them what they should be doing. Most Americans, on the other hand, would just as soon not have the government involved in their lives in every way. We had a president who was known as the "Great Delegator," and it suited most of us fine—even if he slept on the job. Delegation preserves the notion of self-determination among followers. But delegation is also leadership. At the end of the 1980s, there was no Berlin Wall, and there was no Cold War, and no Soviet Union. Reagan was able to concentrate his conscious efforts on defeating Communism. Not a bad accomplishment between naps.

(7) Saying "No! You Do It" Can Help Others

Saying "No" to certain obligations, to certain rocks and mountains, will, as a matter of course, make the weight of the rocks fall upon the shoulders of others. This need not be an exercise in shirking duties. Quite to the contrary, saying "No", and quitting the performance of tasks can be an affirmative statement that we have confidence that those who will come after us can and will carry on successfully. We don't have to be the one to do it, "in order to have it done right." There are no indispensable persons. We are not indispensable.

Psychologist Frank Quinn has been counselling families for a quarter century. He has dealt time and again with the consequences of parents' refusals to let their children grow and learn to deal with life on their children's own terms. They don't let go, and in the process they kill an essential spirit of self-worth and accomplishment. Such a spirit is needed for independent successful accomplishments in adult life. Quinn documents many case studies in his manuscript, "Fat Dogs Don't Run No Rabbit—Hungry Dogs Do." So too, an over guidance of subordinates stymies their opportunities to learn and grow.

This overbearing control activity inevitably leads to crises of succession when health problems, old age, or death intervenes with those who have come to believe that they are indispensable. With no tried- and-experienced leaders at lower spots within an organization, the belief may become at least temporarily a self-fulfilling prophesy.

But parents and organizational leaders do not have to completely let go of the rock and the mountain to make their own journey much easier and to instruct others for their journey as well. Parents and leaders can accomplish these goals by willingly delegating more and more rock pushing tasks to children and to subordinate workers.

Through my children's early teen years, my wife and I played the inevitable role of taxi driver. While it was an expected obligation of parenthood, the role often did become a chore. It was a joy when each child became 16-years-old and received a driver's license. We had both performed the role of driver-teacher as we supervised each child during the learner's permit stage. When the license was granted, we felt we should accept the determination of the state evaluators. Our children were deemed qualified to drive a car.

The children were given a gradually expanding right to drive a family car. They agreed to inform us of their travel itinerary each time they took-off during their first year behind the wheel. They also agreed to share in paying a portion of the extra increment in our increased car insurance payment. When the (fortunately) few traffic tickets (and more commonly parking tickets) came, the children paid the fines in full, and in one case attended the traffic school. After each left home for college, we felt confident that they were prepared to be responsible car-owners and operators—as soon as they agreed they could handle the financial obligations without hurting their studies. Of course, the experience of letting our children drive was laden with many doubts, and a normal amount of worries and fears—but that is also part and parcel of the delegation experience generally.

Fred credits much of his successful group law practice to the mentoring of attorney Lewis K. Howe. Howe hired him for his staff and paid him a salary along with bonuses to conduct litigation. Howe set down some basic rules on accepting clients and the use of the firm's expenses in cases, and then he turned him loose. Fred struggled through the various stages of a case. He soon found that he loved to make arguments in court and in front of judges in chambers. When he decided to venture out on his own and form his own firm, he purposely sought as his first partner a lawyer who loved to do research and to write pleadings. But soon there were new junior partners as well. While Fred continues to enjoy his courtroom presentations, he senses that the growth of the firm would be stifled if he insisted on making all the arguments in court—even in the major cases. He had to shake-off a feeling that he was the best and therefore he had to do the job personally. He let the new younger, inexperienced lawyers begin to run with the cases—to accept cases and to handle all aspects of the cases including arguments in court. If the junior partner started a case, no matter how important it was, the junior partner handled the entire case, even if it went to the state supreme court for oral arguments.

The junior partners were not given card blanche as they were also held responsible for results. Fred monitors case conclusions and these are tied to a system of bonus compensation. For most of these lawyers, the responsibility has been seized upon eagerly. The delegation reaches the full staff as well. Michael, for his part, has been totally delighted that Fred has allowed him to participate in all aspects of a case expect those demanding action by a member of the bar. He does research and he writes pleadings which are reviewed but most often left unchanged by the attorneys.

In one situation one of the firm's younger attorneys could not meet the demands of all aspects of the job. After review, he was encouraged to pursue work elsewhere. Actually Fred reviewed his work, and he found many strong points that allowed him to give an honest and very supportive recommendation for a job in a firm that did another kind of client work not demanding frequent trials. That lawyer has prospered with his new firm.

By letting go of some of his firm's court work and other aspects of cases as well, Fred has been able to move away from being a slave to a calendar set by others. He has been freed to work more at his own pace—which can at times be quite frenetic. In this new freedom, he has been able to explore many more roles which he can play in the growing firm. He has become a real estate and building expert as he has directed the purchase and expansion of facilities for his firm. He has been able to devote attention to service work with students at the local college of law. He sees long term advantages for his firm in this work. For instance, he uses the experience as an implicit way to screen potential new junior partners for the future, and also to build bridges to other law firms. But mostly, Fred senses a lot of immediate personal satisfaction in these interactions.

Additionally, by delegating tasks, Fred has time for bar association activities, as he will be the vice president of the county organization next year. Moreover, in addition to saving extra moments for family life, Fred has been able to squeeze in two nights a week for a city recreational league basketball team, and also time to be a booster an active fan of his favorite team, the UNLV Running Rebels. He'll always be a student-fan in his heart. He never gives up hope that the Rebels will again achieve the magic of their years in the 1980's.

There are many books about delegation, and they spell-out the specifics of the processes and methods that make delegation successful. However, here it can be stated with conviction that delegation works. It may not be easy to accomplish, and it may require great patience and also considerable faith. Indeed, it might require at least a temporary suspension of high standards of perfection that might have guided you in your own work. But in the long run, delegation is necessary for any organization that expects to outlive its immediate incumbent members. And delegation sure beats the alternative—heavy rock pushing until your work days are over.

(8) Really saying "No" to the Work Jobs—Retire

Remember, unlike Sisyphus, we are not condemned for eternity, there will come a time when we can do something else, and a time when we can rest. The time can be of our own choosing. On the one hand, we can move to another job, on the other, we can also retire. We should look at retirement with some thought beforehand. The option becomes viable under certain circumstances. We may have a choice. It can be a good choice if:

- We have a program of helpful activity we can do in retirement.
- We can engage in a program of travel with a purpose.
- We can truly enjoy the rest, even idle rest.
- We can use the time to give happiness to others.
- We have the financial ability to live the retirement life we wish to have.

Sisyphus was stuck on one mountain with his large rock. In reality, we too will probably be stuck on some mountain until...

We'll, until we die. Sisyphus was not able to look forward to death as an ultimate relief from his problems. It may not be much consolation, but we are allowed to look forward to a rest at the end of our journey. At the same time, that very real prospect should give us cause to wonder how we can best live the rest of our limited days. That prospect should motivate us to adjust our tasks and our manner of climbing and pushing, so that the mountains do not conquer our spirit during our life journey. Our limited time should also push us toward the rocks and the mountains that are best suited for our lives. Yet all the mountains we can consider may eventually exhaust our physical or spiritual tools, and we will want to walk away from them all while we still have days left. At least we can walk away from the heavy rock of employment. Sisyphus did not have a choice about retirement. We do.

The choice of retirement is often made for us as a condition of employment on a particular mountain. Sometimes our health mandates the choice. But for most of us the choice can be freely made. We can continue working at some job, or we can stop working all together. One survey found that 40% of retirees consciously chose to retire because of their personal desire to do so.

The choice of retirement from a work life presents us with great opportunities and also saddles us with new challenges. The challenges may not be the same rocks we have been pushing, but in some cases they may be new rocks. Where we have a choice we should consider several things.

Many persons who have been worn down by rock pushing struggles need and truly welcome a time of rest and idleness during which they can move slowly through their days just watching the world pass by. Their Sisyphean struggles have earned them the right to do so.

Others, especially those who have been personally engaged in the mountain climbing, those who in Dubin's terms made the rock pushing their "Central Life Interest," find a transition to idleness very dissatisfying. For these people a successful retirement (given that they are healthy) will probably require a transition to another type of activity. That activity, though it may involve some rock pushing, need not be a Sisyphean exercise. The activity can be truly one of choice, it can be pursued with an open time schedule, with a lack of obligations, and with no periodical reports that must be reviewed by superiors. The free style of activity need not be subject to systems such as Management By Objectives.

The new activity of retirement can present great opportunities for life satisfaction. It can unleash creative energies that had been held down beneath the rocks. For many persons, the years of life after employment allow a rekindling of unfulfilled youthful urges to paint, to write, to make music, to read and study, to learn about places and people through travel, and to engage in certain social activities. Many retired seniors become involved in political activity. Some turn to volunteer activities helping other people. The largest numbers of people joining the Peace Corps are pre-career youth. The second largest group are retirees. Free time activity also allows for those who have had "busy" careers to revive and expand creative social interactions with family and non-work related friends.

In our "Solution I list" we saw the rock and the journey up the mountain as an opportunity for us to have a "place" and an "identity" in life. Work-life and other rock obligations provide us with an element of integration of our self and our society. Retirement, like unemployment, can take these things away from us. Many persons can live well without satisfying these needs through activity. They can happily withdraw into a pleasant isolation.

However, too many others find retirement to be a time of lonely emptiness without new involvements. So these retirees should consider making a transition to personal and social activity that can allow them to retain their sense of their social existence and personal worth.

Preretirement planning becomes an important tool for those who have been personally engaged with their work rock. A big part of preretirement planning comes implicitly years before leaving a job. Whether activity off the job is one's "Central Life Interest" or not, the activity helps one in coping with the struggles of the mountain, but it also prepares a person for life without the rock and mountain of work. Retirement is a great time to develop and expand existing hobbies. However, it has been found that it is much more difficult to begin brand new hobbies after retirement begins.

We are very fortunate in that the Sisyphean work tasks that are put upon our shoulders are not burdens for eternity. If we can ponder well the lessons presented in the "Solutions" above, our lifelong Sisyphean struggles can be enjoyed with a realization that the struggles are part of our humanity.

(9) We Get to Escape All the Rocks and All the Uphill Pushing— Someday

The story has been told many times before. It appears in Kushner's books. A stranger from another land visits the Earth where he meets a human being. In the course of their conversation, the human being tells the stranger about death and the reality of dying that comes for all human beings. The stranger knows nothing about this, as where he comes from there is no death. Perhaps in his universe, there was also a Sisyphus. But there Sisyphus never got around to releasing Thanatos from his captivity. As the human being describes his fate, the stranger begins to shed tears.

"Don't cry for us my stranger friend," says the human creature. "It is part of our nature. It is not all that bad."

"But my human friend, I am not crying for you. I am crying for me and my people." Like Sisyphus, the stranger really could not quit his arduous tasks of rock pushing. The stranger could not enjoy a final time of rest, a time when the struggles would all be over. But also for the stranger, life and all its time was meaningless, hence any struggles—and there were also struggles—were meaningless. Without end, time was not a limited resource. Any economist can tell us that a commodity that is in unlimited supply cannot have value. For the stranger, goals as well as accomplishments were of no meaning. Mananas without end, meant todays of no purpose.

Other than providing an essential driving force that shoves us toward results, the limited time that is provided by the mandatory time of rest at the end of our rock pushing has other values as well. Retirement allows us to escape the demands of others that we push and push and push. A time of total rest allows other escapes. It allows escapes from tiredness, restricted mobility, myriad pains, and endless days without a focus upon meaningful futures. **The limited days we have should propel us to reflect on the joys of our journeys taken**. But it does allow us to find escapes in hopes for reuniting with friends and relatives who are already at rest, and the faith to be united with the ultimate Creative Force of our universe. With the escapes, we can experience a finality as we pass the torch onto our successors who remain behind. Finally we can let them go up the mountains.

The journey with acceptance, adjustments, restructuring and reassessments is always one filled with choices—from the beginning to the end. We have choices. The victory of pushing the rock **over the top** of the mountain peak, the victory of passing the torch onward comes by choice.

Country music singer George Jones poignantly brings the message clearly to us in the words of his song, "I've Had Choices." Jones looks back upon his time with much regret, as he had been told about "right and wrong," but often he would not listen. Now as his mountain trail is narrowing and his journey is coming to a conclusion, he feels that the consequences of the choices are resting heavy on his shoulders. "If I'da only listened, I wouldn't be here today—living and dying with the choices I've made." Jones indicates that if he could now just go back, "Oh, Lord knows I'd run." But still George Jones has a trail in front of him, and still, while he breathes the air of the Earth, he still has more choices.

Choice means freedom. It is of no small notice that only one part of the United States Constitution guarantees us personal freedom in our relationships with all other people. The rest of the Constitution deals only with our relationships with governments and public officials. The Thirteenth Amendment proclaims that we are free, and that neither government nor any other person may violate that freedom and our capacity to make choices. In America there can be no involuntary servitude.

"Neither slavery nor involuntary servitude, except as a punishment for crime whereof the party shall have been duly convicted, shall exist within the United States, or any place subject to their jurisdiction."

(10) When You Have Asserted Your Ultimate Freedom from the Rocks and the Mountains: Celebrate!

When You Push the Rock Over the Top: Celebrate, Celebrate, Celebrate, Celebrate, Celebrate. And so with Bob's words from the day (actually he was assisted by John as he left early in the afternoon) on the chart, we readied ourselves for the night of nights. We were going to **Celebrate!**

Table 4. REASSESS THE JOURNEY

1. Just SAY "NO" "That's not my mountain, I shall not push that rock!"
2. CHOOSE your mountain with care.
3. Find ANOTHER MOUNTAIN. Find ANOTHER ROCK.
4. DON'T PUSH other's rocks FOR THEM.
5. Think of OTHER PATHWAYS.
6. DELEGATE: LET others GO. Let others GROW.
7. Saying, "NO YOU DO IT," can help others.
8. RETIRE from the WORK of rock pushing mountain journeys.
9. REST FROM IT ALL—someday.
10. When you have asserted your freedom from rocks and mountains—CELEBRATE!!!!!

CHAPTER 7

MARDI GRAS—THE ULTIMATE CELEBRATION—LAISSEZ LES BON TEMPS ROULE

The celebration of celebrations—Nothing as big this side of the rainbow.

To cope with the rocks and the mountains, we must celebrate moments of our lives everyday. We must celebrate with routine rituals—reading a good book, watching a movie or a favorite television show, playing with the kids, phoning a friend. We should also consider taking breaks from the routines and the daily rituals and devoting time to special celebrations for special occasions that can be remembered and savored for many days, weeks, and even years into the future.

I felt that I had earned the right for such a personal celebration, for such a personal reward. For four days I had devoted my energies to a seminar in a far-off city. I had a sense that what I shared with Fred's group of colleagues and friends was valuable information. The group (I was hopeful) felt the same, that for them their time, attention, and participation had resulted in the acquisition of some useful insights for their work and for their lives. The group sensed too that they had earned time that could be devoted to a special celebration, a big celebration, a celebration to be remembered.

In their daily lives, I urged them to always welcome their own "Miller Time." But for this week, on this Saturday, they should welcome the greatest celebration of them all: Mardi Gras in New Orleans: Let the Good Times Roll.

So, after we took a short snack-break, we were on the street car headed toward Canal Street and the parade of the Bacchus Krewe. Later we were going to roam Bourbon Street and the French Quarter and then at 10 p.m. go to the Hilton Ball Room for the King Bacchus Ball. All the time we would be taking in the sights of floats and krewes, the "Indians," and the bands, and the revelers, and we would be shouting and singing and marching along with the throng.

Bob had left us in the mid-afternoon, as he was part of the Bacchus Krewe, and he was helping get the float ready, and especially he was getting ready to ride on the float in his special costume. He had arranged for us to make a drop-by walk-through (should I say shove-through) appearance at the ball in the Hilton.

Mardi Gras celebrations are held worldwide as a time of merriment between the season that ends with the Day of Epiphany (Three Kings day, January 6) and the beginning day of Lent, Ash Wednesday. Mardi Gras means "Fat Tuesday" and it connotes the final day of the celebration, a day in the religious calendar which is known has Shrove Tuesday. At midnight on Shrove Tuesday, Lent begins and the masses are "supposed" to go into a somber 40-day period of penitence as they await Good Friday and holy Easter Sunday. So if things are going to close down for 40 days, party on, party strong.

The first New Orleans Mardi Gras celebration was held by the Spanish in 1669, but it was not the first American Mardi Gras. That honor is kept by the city of Mobile, Alabama which was also settled by the

Spanish in the 17th Century. Nonetheless, along with Rio De Janeiro, New Orleans vies for the title of having the biggest and most festive Mardi Gras celebration each year.

Mardi Gras celebrations bring a million visitors to the city of 500,000. Most are looking to get some free "beads" and also a chance to find a restroom.

The distinguishing feature of the New Orleans Mardi Gras is the parade. Over 200 parades are held throughout the season with a dozen or more being held on each of the final days. The parades have as many as 15 floats along with bands and other entertainers. The parades take different routes, so there is one on each major street in the central city area each day for the weeks before Fat Tuesday. The biggest ones go down Canal Street, sometimes referred to as the widest city street in America.

The very decorative themed-floats are constructed and operated by "krewes," or private clubs. Members of krewes pay to be in the club and to ride in the parade. The money is used to build the floats and also to conduct the fancy costume balls. In 2001, 17000 people participated in krewes building and riding on floats. Not only did they contribute money to build the floats, but they also had to reach into their own pockets for an average of $500 each to purchase trinkets called "throws." As they ride on the floats they toss the trinkets which include items like dolls, toy guns, silk panties, faux pearls and, of course, doubloons, and beads of various colors, lengths and sizes.

The most heard phrase along the parade routes is "Throw Me Something, Mister." The krewe member looks about the crowd and if he sees a pleasant looking person (woman) he stares suggesting, "Of course, I will if..." This eye contact bartering may lead to a young lass showing a bit of private flesh to the krewe in exchange for a "throw." Much teasing goes back and forth. Also there is much scrambling for beads when they are thrown. Shoving and pushing and even fights break out for the items that may retail for 25 cents a string.

Marching along side of the floats or riding the floats may be one or more Black Mardi Gras "Indians," a special feature of the celebration. These participants represent a unique subculture of the local population. Tradition has it that they dressed up in full body costumes of feathers, leather and paint to hide their identities and also their race. They wished to freely enjoy the festivities of the parades in a past time when rigid rules of racial segregation governed the Mardi Gras celebration as well as other aspects of social life in the American South.

We cheered loudly as we saw Bob's Bacchus Krewe coming around the corner of St. Charles Street onto Canal Street. It was preceded by two "Indians" mingled amongst members the Southern University Jaguar Marching 100. We kept yelling "Throw Me Something, Mister." It wasn't yet Fat Tuesday, but it was Saturday night, and the crowd was dense and anxious for excitement.

We allowed the force of the crowd to push us behind the Bacchus Krewe float and at Bourbon Street we naturally went stage right. As we continued our walk down the middle of the street, we acquired drinks in our hands and we observed the balconies. These were also packed with painted people likened to the krewes. They also gazed over gatherings of women (of all ages) who yelled out "Throw me something, Mister," and made teasing gestures toward their clothing, and indicated that a sting of beads might be worth a kiss.

Our wanderings seemed to go block after block, when we noticed that it was 10:30 p.m. and we ventured toward the Riverwalk and the Hilton Hotel. The ball was another mass of humanity, but somehow with liquid re-vitalization we "coped" through the events watching one of Bob's fellow krewe members being crowned "King Bacchus of the Crescent City." At 1 a.m. the ball broke down and everyone starting yelling, "Time to Get You Booties Back on Bourbon Street, Party On, Party Strong." Somehow we were able to struggle (the cool air helped matters) a mile or so in the streets and found a cab at just about 2 a.m. It took us back to the Mansion de 'le Jardin where with smiles on our faces (we had also taken some beads to throw) we drank and talked until after 4 a.m.

Three nights later the festivities abruptly ended at Midnight with the Bells of the St. Louis Cathedral in Jackson Square sounding the death knell for the year's Mardi Gras. It was Lent. By the end of Fat Tuesday we were well engrossed in our jobs once more in Springfield, Collegeville, and Las Vegas—a quite unlikely venue to be spending the somber days of Lent. But in those days of Lent we could carry forth dreams and memories of a night of Mardi Gras.

Though the party was over, it remained in our minds ready to be retrieved when at some future moment, at the many future moments, when we needed to have our celebration once more. **We were Over The Top!**

Laissez les bon temps rouler. And so we did!

THE SUPPORTING CHARACTERS

Billy Gamble: The Narrator, a Professor at the University of Nevada, Las Vegas.
Larry Bach: Practicing Dentist in Springfield, Wisconsin. Native of Collegeville, Graduate of Allegheny College and University of Missouri Dental College.
Eddie Bauschard: A New Orleans criminal defense attorney. Graduate of Loyola University of New Orleans and Tulane Law School.
Elizabeth Boatright: Financial Clerk, Walker and Hardcastle, Law Associates, Las Vegas, Nevada.
Jennifer Gamble: Graduate of Purdue University and the University of Nevada, Reno. Counselor with Residential Life, Loyola University.
John Hall: Member of Walker and Hardcastle, specializes in criminal defense cases. Graduate of Gannon College and University of Mississippi Law School.
Tom Hardcastle: Principal in Walker and Hardcastle, specializes in workmen's compensation cases. Graduate of Kalamazoo College and the University of California Law School in Berkeley.
Mary Holmes: Office Manager, Walker and Hardcastle, Law Associates. 14 years.
Paul Lawrence: Member of Walker and Hardcastle, concentrates on medical malpractice and other civil law cases. Graduate of University of Iowa, and University of Michigan Law School.
Roger Lowe: Marketing Consultant with "The Cow and the Lantern" Irish Pub, Collegeville, Michigan, formerly owner-manager of High Fashions by Lowe,

Collegeville. Native of Chicago, Graduate of the Business College, Loyola University, Chicago.

Sandy Mitchell: Office Manager, O'Leary and Lawder, Attorneys at Law, Las Vegas.

Michael Rashid Russell: Graduate of University of Nevada, Las Vegas, and member of N.C.A.A. Final Four basketball team. Formerly, personnel specialist with Los Amigos Casino Properties, now para-legal with Walker and Hardcastle Law Associates, and student at University of Nevada, Las Vegas, Law College.

Bob Walker: Member of Walker and Hardcastle Law Associates, Graduate of Eureka College, and Loyola Law College of New Orleans, specializes in automobile accident cases.

Frederick Walker: Principal in Walker and Hardcastle Law Associates, Las Vegas. Graduate of University of Nevada, Las Vegas, and Tulane University Law School.

Shirley Wicker: Runner, Walker and Hardcastle, Law Associates.

BIBLIOGRAPHY

Albom, Mitch. 1997. Tuesday's with Morrie. New York: Doubleday.

Camus, Albert. 1942. The Myth of Sisyphus. Paris: Gallimard.

Carlzon, Jan. 1987. Moments of Truth. Cambridge, MA: Ballinger.

Coonradt, Charles. 1997. The Game of Work. Park City, UT: Game of Work.

Dubin, Robert. 1992. Central Life Interest. New Brunswick, NJ: Transaction Publ.

Fisher, Seymour and Rhonda L. Fisher. 1993. The Psychology of Adaptation to Absurdity. Hillsdale, NJ: L. Earlbaum Associates.

Fulghum, Robert. 1988. All I Really Need to Know I Learned in Kindergarten. New York: Villard Books.

Harold Garfinkle. 1967. Studies in Ethnomethodology. Englewood Cliffs, N.J.: Prentice Hall.

Grant, Michael and John Hazel. 1973. Who's Who in Classical Mythology. London: Weidenfeld and Nicolson.

The Brothers Grimm. 1992. Fairy Tales. New York: Knopf.

Horace. 1961 Odes (translation by Helen Henze). Norman: University of Oklahoma Press.

Howe, George and G. A. Harrer. 1970. A Handbook of Classical Mythology. Detroit: Gale Research.

Ivker, Robert S. and Edward H. Zorensky. 1998. Thriving. New York: Three Rivers Press.

Kaplin, Roy. 1978. Lottery Winners. New York: Harper and Row.

Kushner, Harold S. 1981. Why Bad Thing Happen to Good People. New York: Schocken Books.

Liddy, G. Gordon. 1980. Will. New York: St. Martin's Press.

Lynch, Jerry and Chungliang Al Huang. 1998. Working Out, Working Within. New York: J. P. Tarcher.

MacCulloch, Canon John Arnott. 1964. The Mythology of All Races, v. i. New York: Cooper Square.

Peter, Lawrence J. and Raymond Hull. 1969. Peter Principle.
New York: W. Morrow.

Peter, Lawrence J. 1971. Peter Prescription. New York: W. Morrow.

Presthus, Robert. 1978. The Organizational Society. New York: St. Martin's Press.

Quinn, Frank. 2001. Fat Dogs Don't Run No Rabbits. Columbia, SC: Manuscript.

Sharkansky, Ira. 1970. Routines of Politics. New York: Van Nostrand.

Singer Jerome L. 1966. Daydreaming. New York: Random House.

Thompson, William N. 2001. Gambling in America: An Encyclopedia of History, Issues and Society. Santa Barbara, Denver and Oxford: ABC-Clio.

Thompson, William N. and Michele Comeau. 1992. Casino Customer Service: WIN WIN Game. New York: Gaming and Wagering Business.

Vonnegut, Kurt. 1950. Welcome to the Monkey House. New York: Dell.

Webster's New World Dictionary. 1975. Springfield, MA: Merriam-Webster, Inc.

Webster's Ninth New Collegiate Dictionary. 1990. Springfield, MA: Merriam-Webster, Inc.

About The Authors

William N. Thompson (on right) is a professor of public administration at the University of Nevada, Las Vegas. Dr. Thompson received his undergraduate education and master's degrees at Michigan State University, and his doctoral studies were completed at the University of Missouri-Columbia in 1972. His degrees are in political science. He is a widely recognized authority on the gambling industry worldwide. His seven previous books examine public policy pertaining to as well as operational aspects of gambling. His research endeavors have taken him to over 500 casinos on five continents. He has also been a consultant for numerous casinos including ones on Native American lands. Additionally, he has advised governments and citizens' groups on issues in this field.

Bradley Lawler Kenny (on left) is a practising attorney in Las Vegas, Nevada. He is licensed to practice in Nevada courts as well as the U.S. District Court in Nevada and the U.S. Ninth Circuit Court of Appeals. Attorney Kenny received his bachelor's degree from Eureka College in Illinois. His Juris Doctor degree was granted by Loyola University in New Orleans in 1993. He also attended the University of Nevada, Las Vegas for postgraduate work in economics. Kenny currently serves as a member of the Board of Directors for the Clark County Bar Association and as a member of the Nevada Trial Lawyers Association. Over The Top is his first book.

Printed in the United States
1306000003B/397-462

9 781403 391360